The Prime Ministers Who Never Were

The Prime Ministers Who Never Were

Edited by Francis Beckett

First published in Great Britain in 2011 by
Biteback Publishing Ltd
Westminster Tower
3 Albert Embankment
London
SE1 7SP

ISBN 978-1-84954-023-0

10 9 8 7 6 5 4 3 2 1

A CIP catalogue record for t̶h̶i̶s̶ ̶b̶o̶o̶k̶ ̶i̶s̶ ̶a̶v̶a̶i̶l̶a̶b̶l̶e̶ ̶f̶r̶o̶m̶ ̶t̶h̶e̶ ̶B̶r̶i̶t̶i̶s̶h̶ Library.

Set in Adobe Garamond
Printed and bound in Great ̶B̶r̶i̶t̶a̶i̶n̶ ̶b̶y̶
CPI Mackays, Chatham ME̶5̶ ̶8̶T̶D̶

Contents

Foreword

During my active political career I used to believe, adapting the words of a nineteenth-century presidential candidate in the United States, that I would rather people wondered why I was *not* Prime Minister than why I *was*.

At that time I therefore believed it was better to be Foreign Secretary or Chancellor of the Exchequer than Prime Minister – to *do* something rather than *be* something. Now, however, I feel it is better to be Prime Minister because you can then ensure that all the other ministers do the right thing.

So I believe that not only the Labour Party but also Britain lost a great deal by not having John Smith as Prime Minister – he was a man of great intellectual strength and pragmatism, a good deal more than Hugh Gaitskell who was another personality with the characteristics for the job.

I very much welcome this series of counterfactual essays, because we can learn a good deal from informed speculation about what might have been.

Denis Healey
February 2011

Introduction

Individuals make history. There's no inevitability, and everything's up for grabs. Marx was right about lots of things, but he was wrong about that. As Karl Popper wrote in *The Poverty of Historicism*, 'the belief in historical destiny is sheer superstition, and there can be no prediction of the course of human history by scientific or any other rational methods.'

I'm quite pleased about that. It used to worry me back in the seventies, when Marxism was fashionable among the children of the sixties. I used to think: if the triumph of socialism is inevitable, why bother to work for it? I was never a Marxist because I found it demotivating. Scientific socialism is as false a god as God.

I'm even more pleased now, because if history were a stately process of pre-ordained forces, this book would be pointless, and I've had wonderful fun doing it. History is changed by all sorts of things, and one of them is which human being gets to the top of the tree. Supposing the American people had got the president they narrowly voted for in 2000, whose name was Al Gore, a great many things would be different.

How different? Well, one of the contributors to this book thinks the Second World War would never have happened if his man had become Prime Minister, and he makes a pretty good case for it. That's how different it could be.

Each of these chapters describes a premiership that never came about – but might easily have happened. The criteria for inclusion: the person never attained the top job, but there was a particular moment when, had the chips fallen slightly differently, he would have done.

J. R. Clynes lost the Labour leadership to Ramsay MacDonald by a paper-thin margin; if he had won it, he and not MacDonald would have become Labour's first Prime Minister. Lord Halifax had the opportunity to take the premiership in 1940 instead of Winston Churchill; he turned it down. In January 1957 the Tory grandee Lord Salisbury, who could not pronounce the letter R, invited the Cabinet into his room one by one and asked: 'Is it Wab or Hawold?' The smart money was on them all saying Wab, but the majority said Hawold, and so Harold Macmillan it was. Neil Kinnock's election defeat in 1992 was narrow and unexpected. And so on.

I've been strict about gatekeeping. Just being the leader of the Conservative or Labour Party was not enough to get in, because it didn't mean you were in with a shout of getting to 10 Downing Street. There was never a moment when anyone thought, dear me, Iain Duncan Smith might become Prime Minister sometime soon.

Even leading your party into an election didn't hack it. There was never any prospect that Arthur Henderson was going to lead Labour to victory in 1931, nor that William Hague might win for the Conservatives in 2001, so you won't find them here. Michael Foot gains admittance, not because he led Labour in the 1983 general election – everyone knew he would lose by a landslide, and he did. He's in because there was a real prospect of him beating James Callaghan in the very tight Labour leadership contest of 1976, when Labour was in power.

At first I planned to include Gordon Brown (stands against Blair for the leadership in 1994, wins, and become Prime Minister in 1997) but he was grimly determined to render himself ineligible for inclusion in this book, and succeeded in doing so by actually becoming Prime Minister in 2007.

These criteria explain why there are no women on my list. I wanted to have at least one, because I know a lot of people who will be very sniffy about their absence, but she had to fit the criteria. I tried hard to construct the moment when Barbara Castle or Shirley Williams might have become Prime Minister had circumstances been different, but it isn't there.

Getting to be Prime Minister is more often than not a matter of chance. It's quite likely that neither Harold Wilson nor Tony Blair would ever have got the job had it not been for the sudden, early and unexpected deaths of their respective predecessors, Hugh Gaitskell and John Smith.

The authors of this book have asked themselves questions like: what shape would the welfare state and the Cold War have taken if the Prime Minister had been Herbert Morrison instead of Clement Attlee? What if the Eurosceptic Butler had become Prime Minister instead of the Euro-enthusiast Harold Macmillan? The uncompromising Eurosceptic Hugh Gaitskell instead of the sophisticated compromiser and Euro-enthusiast Harold Wilson? How would our present life be different without New Labour – a name we would never have heard if either Kinnock or Smith had become Prime Minister and not Tony Blair?

Does it matter? Yes, it matters a lot. Understanding what might have happened, how things might have been better (or worse) if we had taken a slightly different path, is what will help us to do things better next time. What might have happened matters almost as much as what really did happen. Some serious historians look down their noses at counterfactual history, and most politicians regard it as suitable only for butterflies like me, but I maintain that counterfactual history isn't just fun. It IS fun – much more fun than the real thing. But it also matters. It can teach us things that we will never learn from the dull facts.

Each of the chapters in this book describes events that really might have happened – and almost did.

Francis Beckett
February 2011

Prime Minister Austen Chamberlain splits the Tories

Stephen Bates

Rarely can there have been a man for whom a glittering political career has been so ordained from birth as Austen Chamberlain. And rarely has there been a senior politician whose character less equipped him to reach the heights for which he had been groomed and to which he and his family assumed he was entitled.

It was not exactly a bad career: Chancellor of the Exchequer a week before his fortieth birthday, later Secretary of State for India and Foreign Secretary, and altogether a minister for more than twelve years during forty-five years as an MP.

Yet more was always expected of him and the premiership was what many saw as his due and destiny. Like several others, though, who thought similarly of themselves – Anthony Eden and Gordon Brown come to mind – Chamberlain's ambition ended in dust and ashes.

Photographs of Austen Chamberlain and his father Joseph show an eerie similarity. Both are pictured outside the same wrought iron gates at the House of Commons. Both are tall, lean men; both wear identical clothes: grey frock coats, white waistcoats and wing collars. Both have buttonholes; both slicked-back hair parted on the left; both monocles in the right eye. If there is a difference, it is that Austen has the more patrician and haughty expression.

Joseph, the prosperous screw manufacturer who became lord mayor of Birmingham at the age of thirty-seven and pioneered a programme of municipal improvement locally – 'gas and water socialism' – and political radicalism nationally, would end up wrecking both main parties. As a Liberal he fell out with Gladstone over home rule for Ireland and then as a Conservative Unionist twenty years later brought electoral disaster on his party by calling for the imposition of import tariffs to replace the free trade on which British prosperity was thought to rest.

As a force of political nature, Joseph was dynamic but mistrusted: not necessarily the recipe for successful leadership. But if he fell short of the highest office to which his talents might have taken him, then his eldest son Austen – whose mother, Joseph's first wife, died giving birth to him in 1863 – was destined from childhood to carry the dynasty onwards in politics and government. 'He was,' said Joseph, 'born in a red box, brought up in one and [will] die in one.'

By comparison Austen's younger half-brother Neville was earmarked to carry on the family business, maintain the family fortune and aspire to nothing more than municipal politics.

Austen received a gentleman's education: Rugby and Cambridge, becoming vice-president of the Union debating society, strongly defending his father's policies, before completing his studies with lengthy stays in Paris and Germany to learn the languages and meet influential people such as the Iron Chancellor, Bismarck, with whom he dined. Such privileged progress didn't impress the young man too much: 'one day succeeds another with great monotony,' he wrote. 'A series of such days carry one through the week and the time to write another letter comes round without my having found anything fresh to say.'

He and Neville then found time to deplete the family fortunes with an unsuccessful investment venture in sisal production in the Bahamas – the only commercial, indeed non-political, occupation in Austen's entire life – before he found a safe seat, unopposed, as a Liberal Unionist like his father, and a niche in the Commons at the age of twenty-nine in 1892. As political apprenticeships go, it was not strenuous, and he was duly escorted into the chamber with his father on one side and his uncle on the other.

He was a dynastic rather than natural politician: too often 'wooden in face and manner, pompously correct, impeccably virtuous and frigidly uninteresting', as Leo Amery, a political ally, would write in *The Observer* after Chamberlain's death. Being his father's son imposed a burden of expectation on Austen – for him, to support and expound his father's policies and, on the part of others, that he should echo his father's success. Even early on, it was noticed that he lacked his father's drive and fire, that he was lacking the common touch or the energy to push him and party policies forward.

He suffered, one historian has written, 'from being the over-groomed offspring of an outstanding personality'. More waspishly, Arthur Balfour, the Tory leader and Joseph's rival, observed: 'If only Austen was what he looked, how splendid he would be.' Much later, Balfour would speculate on Austen's shortcomings as a politician: 'Don't you think it's because he is a bore?'

That did not prevent a general expectation on his part, his father's part, his party's part, the newspapers' part and the public's part that he was born to rule. The only impediment was that the Chamberlain name was regarded with suspicion, not only among Liberals who saw his father as a traitor, but also among Conservatives who distrusted Joseph Chamberlain and his Liberal Unionist supporters as a disruptive force. If that sense enhanced Austen Chamberlain's political diffidence, it did not stop him climbing seemingly effortlessly ever upward in his career: first the whips' office, then ministerial office at the Admiralty, then financial secretary to the Treasury, and, in 1903, Chancellor of the Exchequer.

Five months earlier, Joseph Chamberlain had launched his campaign for the introduction of protective tariffs on goods imported from outside the Empire, a move which convulsed British politics and contributed to the Conservative and their remaining Liberal Unionist colleagues' landslide defeat in the 1906 election. Austen and his father survived the political massacre but within a few months Joseph suffered a severely disabling stroke which left him partially paralysed and with impaired speech. It was thus left to Austen to emerge from his father's shadow, loyally continue the campaign for Imperial Preference and develop a political career in his own right.

By 1911 both parties were neck and neck in the Commons, in the wake of the constitutional crisis following the Conservative peers' attempt to derail the Liberal government's reforming Budget. Tory MPs grew dissatisfied with Balfour's languid and unenergetic leadership and it was assumed that Austen would succeed him in the ensuing race. Instead, he stood aside, allowing Andrew Bonar Law, a dour Canadian-Scots businessman to become leader.

The First World War saw the Conservatives brought into government and Chamberlain becoming first Secretary of State for India; then once again at the end of the war made Chancellor of the Exchequer in Lloyd George's coalition, responsible for trying to restore the country's economy.

In the spring of 1921, Bonar Law's health failed and he resigned. The two potential candidates to succeed him were Chamberlain, once again, and Lord Curzon, widely disliked for his arrogant and patronising manner. This time, Chamberlain assumed the Conservative leadership. Lloyd George was unpopular, especially with Conservative MPs who feared their party being dragged down in his wake, or, worse, subsumed into what was becoming the Prime Minister's personal party since the Liberals were themselves split between Lloyd George and the former leader, Asquith.

The crunch, when it came in the autumn of 1922, was unforeseen by Chamberlain. Discontent with being tied to the discredited Lloyd George was mounting on the Tory back-benches; there were threats to put up Independent Conservative candidates to oppose the coalition and there was a sense that the government was faltering and could not last much longer. Although several senior Tory members of the coalition insisted that loyalty demanded they continue to support the admin-istration – a drunken Lord Birkenhead berated and insulted MPs who came to see him about withdrawing – Chamberlain could sense the way the wind was blowing.

Nevertheless he hesitated. He did not wish to be disloyal to Lloyd George, whom he had come to rather admire, nor to precipitate the downfall of the government, but by October that year Chamberlain knew that if he was to remain leader he had to lead his party back to independence. He would, he said, be like the Duke of Plaza-Toro in *The Gondoliers*, leading his party from the rear because he found it less exciting.

There was another reason to act, however. Bonar Law was making noises about returning, and there were signs of a challenge from Stanley Baldwin, a rather dull junior minister from a minor Worcestershire business background. He'd been

Chamberlain's junior as financial secretary at the Treasury. Austen did not rate him: 'he is self-centred, selfish and idle… (sly) without a constructive idea in his head,' he would much later write to his sister Ida. But he was astute enough to realise that the revolt might spread.

At a meeting of Tory MPs at the Carlton Club on 19 October, Austen seized the initiative to ditch the coalition, making a speech which for once in his life had the backbenchers cheering. Bolstered by news that an independent Conservative candidate had just been elected in the Newport by-election, defeating Labour who had been expected to win, Chamberlain told his MPs: 'We must regain our own party and form a government at once otherwise we shall be in a damned fix.' An astonished Baldwin rallied the troops by reminding them that they were in thrall to a Prime Minister who was 'a dynamic force … a very terrible thing'. Even Bonar Law chimed in. He offered to resume the leadership, but found little enthusiasm. Of Chamberlain, Birkenhead said, he had undergone a conversion 'swifter than any known in secular or sacred history since Saul of Tarsus changed his name'.

Lloyd George, waiting in Downing Street to hear the outcome of the meeting, was told that the Tories had voted overwhelmingly to split from the coalition. Chamberlain burst in on him excitedly with the news: 'It is of course nonsense to describe it as a Belgravia intrigue or a revolt in the kitchen,' he told the Prime Minister.

Chamberlain had for once acted decisively to quell a revolt in his party, seize the initiative and vault into the prime ministership. He had achieved what his father had never accomplished: the King sent for him to form a government and he himself took up residence at No. 10 – a house, incidentally, that he never liked except for its association with power.

In forming his government, Chamberlain acted to reconcile his party's factions. Baldwin was promoted to Chancellor of the Exchequer and Birkenhead remained as Lord Chancellor. Curzon – who had himself hoped to become Prime Minister – was also left in post as Foreign Secretary. It was, Chamberlain said in his stiff way, an administration of first-rate men, though privately he described Baldwin as a man with 'no House of Commons gifts, can't debate, or think, or act quickly … terribly complacent'. Baldwin though was now too popular and influential within the party to sack, even though Chamberlain thought he was bound to fail as Chancellor.

What the country thought of its new Prime Minister was rather more complicated. In many ways he seemed a throwback to a pre-war era. He still dressed like an Edwardian, in a morning coat, with a wing collar to his shirt. An orchid reposed in his buttonhole and his monocle was screwed firmly to his eye. The French, though appreciative of his excellent foreign language skills, still chuckled at the English 'milord' in London.

Politically, Chamberlain lacked both the common touch and persuasive skills. His oratory was fluent, but stiff and formal. His relations with his constituents in Birmingham were distant and uncomfortable. He could not pretend to have his father's passion and radicalism, and his ideas remained trapped by his family heritage.

Ireland had gone – he grudgingly had to accept that, though he would do nothing to assist the government in Dublin as it fought a civil war against those who would not accept the treaty that gave the twenty-six counties independence.

But there was still the old idea of protective tariffs to pursue. As British industry struggled to revive after the war, he and many members of his government saw protectionism as the only way of ensuring companies could survive. He even wanted to extend tariffs to goods from the Empire, despite warnings about how badly that would be received in Australia and Canada.

Worse, Chamberlain could not see that the old policy of protective tariffs, championed by his father, was now counter-productive to British industrial recovery. It had never been electorally popular and opponents could still make capital with charges that protectionism increased prices at home and thus made the poor poorer still.

'His father's policy has always been to him a hereditary incubus about which he felt dutifully zealous, or dutifully bored,' wrote Leo Amery in his diary, before pinpointing the real tragedy of Chamberlain's short-sightedness: '[it] has never been to him a great object in itself'.

Nevertheless, many Tories agreed with Chamberlain. Baldwin himself became convinced too that tariffs were needed. He told the party conference in Plymouth in 1923 that they would protect jobs: 'To me at least the unemployment prob-lem is the most critical problem of our country. I can fight it. I am willing to fight it. But I cannot fight it without weapons… I have come to the conclusion myself that the only way of fighting this subject is by protecting the home market.'

Baldwin had been scarred by his negotiations with the US government to reschedule Britain's war debts the previous year. Sent to Washington to secure a deal that would involve paying no more than £25 million a year, he had returned with one that amounted to paying £34 million annually for ten years, then £40 million for the next fifty-two, the debt not there-fore scheduled to be paid off before 1984 – an unimaginable burden. There had been a Cabinet revolt, led by Bonar Law, whose throat cancer was slowly killing him and who could no longer speak above a whisper. Chamberlain had sat back, waiting to see which way the wind blew, leaving Baldwin swinging, but ultimately accepting the deal, as did the rest of the Cabinet. Within weeks Bonar Law had resigned, citing his ill health and in no condition to lead a party revolt. By the autumn, he was dead.

Early the following year, Baldwin wanted to go to the country on the policy of protective tariffs, but Chamberlain hesitated. The Labour Party in opposition was already making great play of their charges that tariffs would put up the price of bread and increase hunger. There was already labour unrest.

Prudently, Chamberlain decided not to risk the party's Commons majority in a general election. Privately he insisted it was the government's duty to save the country from socialism and communism. He derided Baldwin's persuasive skills: 'Stanley himself never fires more than a popgun or a peashooter at critical moments and hasn't a ghost of an idea how to fight,' he wrote to his sister.

It was a sentiment that would have astonished many in his party, who themselves had seen Austen at close hand for many years and well understood how little rapport he had among the electorate. It must also have amused his half-brother Neville, by now in the Commons himself, who was busy honing the presentational skills that would stand him in good stead a decade later. As for Baldwin's down-to-earth suavity, Austen was scornful: 'I've heard he practises in front of a mirror,' he said.

Increasingly, however, Austen Chamberlain was bored by domestic considerations. Foreign affairs were what interested him and absorbed his attention. Lord Curzon, who had been a potential rival for the party leadership in 1921, had fallen in behind Chamberlain's leadership and retained his position as Foreign Secretary in his government, privately disdainful though he was of the new Prime Minister: 'Imagine!' he wrote to his wife Grace, 'Our country being led by a Birmingham screw manufacturer. Well, if it is to be so, my country will need me and I must do my duty.'

By early 1925, however, Curzon was waning. He had taken to referring to the French Prime Minister Raymond Poincaré as 'a horrid little man' – symptomatic of his weariness with the world in general – and could barely summon the energy or concentration to work. He was taken ill during a visit to speak to the Cambridge University Conservative Association and died a few days later.

Chamberlain enthusiastically assumed the duties of Foreign Secretary as well as Prime Minister and would in the course of the year spend much time abroad – a novel departure for a Prime Minister – seeking to improve Franco-German relations, an effort which culminated in the famous pact signed at Locarno in October 1925. This foreign triumph expressed agreement between the powers of western Europe (France, Germany, Britain, Belgium and Italy) to refer all disputes to arbitration and never again to resort to war.

Chamberlain was quick to claim credit, though in fact the idea had originally been suggested by the German Foreign Minister Gustav Stresemann, and his efforts were rewarded not only by the Nobel Peace Prize but by the King's award of the Order of the Garter. The Prime Minister, confident of his international diplomacy, returned home saying that Benito Mussolini, the Italian leader, might be a dictator, but he was 'a man with whom business could be done'.

There was no doubt that this foreign triumph – for which Chamberlain deserves to be remembered – distracted his attention from developing problems on the economic front at home. In 1924 Baldwin, with the enthusiastic support of his deputy at the Treasury, Winston Churchill, had urged a return to the Gold Standard, the pre-war Sterling exchange rate, as a sign of the government's determination to recover former economic disciplines and demonstrate Britain's recovery from the strains of the war. Chamberlain agreed and urged Baldwin to act with 'decisive confidence': 'the operation will be found, all things considered, an easy one … if we do not do it, we shall not stay where we were, but inevitably start a retrograde movement.'

The return to the Gold Standard, together with Baldwin's introduction of protective tariffs in the Budget of 1925, had precisely the reverse effects to what was intended. They made exports dearer, so stalling industrial recovery, and imports also more costly, so hitting voters' pockets. The protective tariffs on non-Empire products got bogged down in disputes about how much would be raised and what imports should be exempted: should apples be subject to tariffs? What about tinned salmon? The government had promised that there would be no increase in the cost of basic necessities such as bread, tea and sugar and so, to protect these, tariffs elsewhere had to be raised. The whole thing became a muddle, tariffs costing more to collect than they raised, but also hugely politically damaging because of the Labour Party's accusations that ministers were deliberately increasing the cost of food. Chamberlain, who had supported both moves, appeared not to notice the developing domestic crisis. He was later to bemoan that the government had stumbled over 'a policy of currents and tinned salmon'.

The effect was to stall industrial recovery and institute a cycle of deflation on an already weakened economy. The government lurched into a widening confrontation with trade unions as employers sought to reduce costs by cutting wages and workers attempted to maintain their wages in the face of rising prices. The number of strikes rose to 600 in 1925, involving more than 500,000 workers.

When the miners threatened strike action in early 1925, Chamberlain was finally galvanised into action. For him the threat of Bolshevism was only too apparent, even in the unlikely shape of Ramsay MacDonald.

His fears were bolstered by the dispatches sent back to the Foreign Office from the British embassy in Moscow, by reports arising from MI5, the fledgling domestic secret service, and by police surveillance records of those they deemed suspicious characters. May Day marches were infiltrated by undercover agents, speeches were noted down for signs of subversion and the offices of the Labour and Communist parties were raided.

The reports all pointed in the same direction: subversion was widespread, and revolutionary insurrection, possibly funded with Russian gold, was imminent. A letter, apparently from the Soviet leader Grigori Zinoviev, calling for socialist leaders to foment mutiny in the army was shown to Chamberlain privately by a concerned civil service. How it then found its way to the *Daily Mail* frankly astonished him, but it made him more concerned than ever to show that his government would not falter in the face of industrial disruption. The insurgents must be put in their place and shown who governed Britain.

It would only need a spark, though. He was convinced Labour should never be allowed to take power and that strikes should be forcibly put down in the national interest. Chamberlain had no time for those, even within the Conservative Party, such as Baldwin, who argued that, if Labour was elected, they should be given their chance and that the miners did indeed have a case. This, Chamberlain said, was just weakness and shilly-shallying. Firmness would reward the Conservative Party, dish the remaining Liberals and expose Labour for the quasi-Bolsheviks they were.

Thus it was that the Prime Minister was panicked into a violent reaction when a general strike threatened to bring the country to a halt in the summer of 1925. It was indeed a bloody affair. The strike was triggered by the decision of the coal owners to cut pay and increase hours. With other workers from the transport and railway unions threatening to join in, Chamberlain set the government's face against any compromise or mediation.

The employers must be supported, he said and miners must make sacrifices for economic recovery just like everyone else. He did not accept that the government had any role in mediating a trade dispute, but he was quite prepared to enforce law and order through the use of troops, who would also be deployed to ensure supplies got through.

This was a stance that was widely popular on the Conservative benches, but much less so in the country at large, which had some sympathy with the miners. Chamberlain, it was said, had never visited a pit or met a miner. His brother Neville once wrote to their sister Ida: 'I don't think myself that A has much sympathy with the working classes; he hasn't been thrown enough into contact with them to know much about them.' He had had no real experience of running a business or employing anyone other than domestic servants. He could not empathise but, worse than that, he saw no need to do so. Now his lack of personal skills was exacerbated by an impatience with the disruption and a fear of anarchy.

It did not help the government that the strike began in the middle of the summer, when coal stocks were low. Ministers nevertheless went on holiday and when they returned in the early autumn, the dispute had still not settled. Now, the triple alliance of the rail, transport and mining unions attempted to turn the screw: their members were desperate, foraging for summer berries in the hedgerows and stealing vegetables from the fields to feed their families, but they had not buckled.

Churchill, by now Home Secretary, argued strongly in Cabinet for the deployment of troops to assist the police and guard convoys of food being brought from the docks. Chamberlain hesitated in the face of a divided Cabinet – Baldwin was urging mediation, or for using government reserves to subsidise miners' wages through the winter – but as he did so, MI5 brought increasingly alarmist reports of Bolshevik conspiracies and plans to subvert the armed forces. The country was in chaos, the newspapers insisted, and Britain was being made a laughing-stock.

Provoked by the accusations of weakness, Chamberlain authorised Churchill to use force, to take over the BBC and close down newspapers giving reports unhelpful to the government.

In unseasonably warm autumn weather late that September, there were a series of flashpoints: police went on strike in Liverpool and refused to supervise pickets at the docks, lead-ing to disorder, widespread looting and, within days, a riot. In London, troops escorting a food convoy through the East End were attacked and retaliated by opening fire, killing five people. In south Wales, police turned a blind eye as strikers attacked a coal owner's mansion. In Yorkshire, a policeman was killed after being hit by a rock.

In the absence of independent news sources, gossip spread rumours that government departments had been attacked and the King had been forced to flee Buckingham Palace (in fact he had merely gone to Scotland for the grouse shooting season).

These reports filtered back to the City of London, causing panic in the markets and a run on the pound. Now the government really was in trouble.

Much against his will, Chamberlain at last sought to mediate, but talks with owners and miners' leaders stalled in mutual intransigence. Then the weather broke: storms and gales swept the country that October and with the cold, dark nights, union members started drifting back to work. The strike had never been solid, but now the trickle became a flood. Last to hold out were the miners, but after Christmas they too were forced back, bitterly accepting the owners' offer not to cut their pay in return for them working an extra hour on each shift. Soon even that agreement was reneged upon and their wages were cut by a shilling a shift.

Chamberlain strove to show this as a victory for common sense and national courage, but the strike had lasted nearly eight weeks and left a legacy of deep bitterness that stretched far beyond the coalfields and into the middle classes, who found that their jobs and wages were also being cut as industrial production waned. It undermined Conservatives' claims to be the embodiment of national unity.

The Prime Minister's authority was also seriously affected as he proved unable to galvanise the country and re-enthuse the national spirit. Tory MPs who had cheered him earlier in the summer now sighed that they had lost the confidence of the country. He was regarded as one of the old, failed gang. The Cabinet was tired and split by personal rivalries. Reeling around the Carlton Club, reeking of brandy, Birkenhead was telling anyone who would listen that Austen was a useless waste of space: 'utterly, utterly useless'. Baldwin was canvassed to mount a leadership challenge. Baldwin: the empty hole at the Cabinet table, the man whose tenure at the Treasury had led to import tariffs and the Gold Standard, the two most disastrous financial decisions the government had made.

What was worse, a general election was due by November 1927 and the government stood to lose its majority. The beneficiaries could only be Labour. A delegation of senior ministers attended on the Prime Minister in Downing Street. Would he stand aside? He would not. He insisted instead that they should show their loyalty to him.

A meeting of Tory MPs and peers was called at the Carlton Club. Chamberlain pleaded for unity but his address was characteristically wooden and his arguments schoolmasterly and hectoring. The meeting ended in uproar and impasse. Even conservative newspapers such as the *Daily Mail*, the *Morning Post* and the *Daily Telegraph* insisted that the government was a rudderless laughing stock and a disgrace: 'Austen Must Go' dominated the headlines. *The Times* warned that the Conservatives were in danger of being out of power for a generation because of the Prime Minister's intransigence and stubbornness.

Then suddenly it was all over. The Prime Minister attempted to call a general election, only to be rebuffed by the King who suggested that the Conservatives were in no position to fight a united campaign and would only open the way to the Socialists. Within a day, doctors had been summoned to Downing Street to examine the Prime Minister and had pronounced him in need of complete rest and recuperation – they had been primed too. He surrendered the reins of power to his brother Neville, the health minister, and retired to a clinic in Switzerland.

Only much later would Austen Chamberlain return to Britain, to his Sussex manor house at Twitts Ghyll near Uckfield, where he busied himself with gardening and creating the most splendid Alpine rockery in the south of England.

From there he would emerge only occasionally in the last ten years of his life, to give interviews denouncing his former colleagues: useless … empty … inert … a cipher … God help us all! And to warn increasingly urgently about the need to re-arm in the face of the rising militarism of Nazi Germany and the looming prospect of a terrible war he would not live to see. But no one paid him any attention, for had he not discredited himself while in government?

Back at Westminster, Ramsay MacDonald and Labour won a landslide victory in October 1927 and entered government for the first time, and with a working majority. The Conservative Party under Neville Chamberlain was split between hardliners, a faction favoured by the leader and by senior figures such as Churchill, and so-called appeasers, more socially progressive, younger MPs such as Harold Macmillan and Robert Boothby, who sought to reconcile the party with working class voters. The Conservatives were still seared and riven by their experience in the general strike.

When the inevitable economic crisis occurred in 1931, with his party's hardliners in the ascendancy, Neville Chamberlain declined to join a government of national unity, insisting that Labour should sort out the mess of its own creation by itself.

Then, at the crisis general election the following year, no party won an overall majority and only after a further election in 1933 were the Conservatives, in alliance with the small rump of surviving Liberal MPs, able to form a coalition government, led by Neville.

That lasted for five years until, following his agreement with the German dictator Hitler, Chamberlain called an autumn general election on the slogan 'He kept us out of War', but was rewarded with only the slenderest of majorities, which would crumble in the face of the German onslaught of 1940.

Austen died in 1937 but he would have been amused and exasperated by his brother's attempts at international mediation. Neville, he sometimes sneered, knew absolutely nothing about foreign affairs.

Prime Minister Clynes stifles the Nazi menace

Phil Woolas

On 30 June 1918, *The Observer* newspaper opined that, within ten years, the Labour Party would form the government and that John Robert Clynes MP, Minister for Food Rationing, would be its Prime Minister. The newspaper was wrong. It was five years not ten.

* * *

Will Thorne MP had been in the game for too long not to spot a plot. It was the Scottish Labour MPs. He saw Jimmy Maxton in animated conference with Emanuel Shinwell by the entrance to the Oriel Room on the Library corridor of the House of Commons, so he knew something was afoot.

Six days earlier, on 15 November 1922, Thorne's protégé Jack Clynes had led the Labour Party to its biggest success to date. By steady, cautious, responsible leadership, the Labour Party had risen from its birth a mere sixteen years previously to the ranks of His Majesty's Official Opposition. Critical to that remorseless rise was the Member for Platting. The youngest of the 1906 intake and President of Thorne's own trade union, the Gasworkers' and General Workers' Union, Clynes was recognised as the greatest strategic talent in the movement, and a man of subtle and poetic intelligence. Combined with that, he was the country's best political organiser; apart from Thorne himself of course.

The Parliamentary Labour Party was due to meet on the lower committee corridor in the House later that day. Everyone assumed that Clynes's re-election as leader (it had been agreed that the title of 'chairman' did not carry sufficient gravitas outside of Parliament) was a formality. Now, Thorne sensed trouble.

Maxton and the 'Red Clydesiders' were impatient for change. And what Socialist could blame them? Of all the country's great cities, Glasgow was suffering the most. Mass starvation was a real possibility and the slums were stirring. Only the previous week, a crowd estimated at 100,000 had seen off the new Socialist MPs from Queen's Square to make the trip to Westminster. As far as they were concerned, they had a mandate.

What Thorne and Clynes had underestimated though was not the impatient enthusiasm of Glasgow but the ambition of a re-tread Member: James Ramsay MacDonald.

Thorne summoned the Messengers; the thirty or so officers of the House who then, as now, wear traditional morning coats and carry silver badges with the symbol of Mercury, God of Messengers. With their help and that of the whips, a last minute ring round was organised of loyal Labour backbenchers to make sure they would be present in the House. Thorne got his black General and Municipal Union minute book and read out the numbers to the Messengers; some were arriving at Euston, St Pancras and King's Cross, a handful at London's other terminals, some were in their digs and unobtainable, some were already in the smoking room and a few were where they shouldn't have been and not reachable. The whips operation was not yet all seeing.

By the time the PLP gathered, Thorne reassured the leader that the rebellion was squashed. MacDonald's coup had been smoked out and exposed. The Labour Party didn't like disloyalty and it liked vanity even less. Clynes had neither; MacDonald had both by the barge load.

When the vote was read out, MacDonald had secured sixty-one to Clynes's seventy-six. Enough of the trade union vote had been mobilised. Clynes, though, had been stung.

The newly re-elected leader did not let the grass grow around his feet. That evening he spoke to the Independent Labour Party, including the new and re-elected MPs, at the Methodist West London Mission at Kingsway Hall, off Holborn. The venue was of Clynes's choosing. He laid out his approach to the victorious gathering. If they maintained loyalty, he promised, he would kiss the King's hand within a year and they, the representatives of the British Labour Movement, would be in power.

John Robert Clynes was born on 27 March 1869 at his parents' terraced home in Back Henshaw Street, Oldham. He was one of ten, eight of whom survived. His father Patrick had emigrated to Lancashire from Ireland. Like hundreds of millions of immigrants before and since, he moved to find work. John, quickly becoming known as Jack, was the fifth child and first son.

His lot was to leave school at ten years old and start work in the mill. A 'Little Piecer', as he and his fellow child-workers were known, was the most dangerous job in the leviathans of the Lancashire cotton industry. Working in bare feet, so as to avoid slipping on the oily mill floor, a piecer's job was to keep the production line going by diving under the machinery, grabbing the broken threads and twisting them together.

Death or mutilation were kept at bay on a whim. The children were chosen to do the job because they were smaller, nimbler and could duck under the crashing spindles with greater agility than the teenagers and adults.

Years later, as Prime Minister of Great Britain, when sitting at the negotiating tables of the world's powers, he would wince at the pain in his feet as the scars of the splinters from the Mill made their lifelong reminder of where 'Little Piecer' had come from. He would have never forgotten in any event.

What was remarkable about Clynes, and the others in Labour's 'Big Five', was that they had all started with nothing. In Clynes's case, as well as starting work at five in the morning at the Dowry Mill in Waterhead, Oldham, bereft of local education, Clynes had scratched around for pennies to buy candle wax to read by, because there was no electricity or gas at the family home in Derker. He secured second-hand copies of Dickens, Ruskin and Shakespeare by earning a penny a week reading the newspapers to the blind at Oldham's new library on Union Street. His favourite place was the co-operative reading room on Lees Road, where he fell in love with literature and the power of words. By the time he was nineteen, he was educated and knowledgeable enough to convince intransigent mill owners that workers too could be civilised.

At twenty-five he was acknowledged as one of the country's most successful trade union organisers. Around 100,000 people joined the General Workers' Union in Lancashire under his leadership at a time when skilled unions and bosses conspired together against the underdog.

He was a short, quiet, contemplative man, completely at ease with himself, never making a statement or a move that wasn't thought through and deliberate. And yet he had an Irish twinkle in his eye. He looked at you as if he knew your thoughts and what you were going to say. It was a character-istic that endeared him to the public because it enhanced the respect they had for him as a man.

Despite his setbacks in standing unsuccessfully three times for the council in Oldham, against the political machinations of no less an opponent than the local Conservative Member of Parliament, Winston Churchill, by age thirty-five he was returned as Labour MP for Miles Platting, just down the road in what had by now become the predominant industrial city in the world, Manchester. He was to serve that constituency without break until 1947.

By then he had already built a formidable political base. Spotted by the founder of the General Workers' Union and the architect of general unionism, Will Thorne, while still a teenager, he quickly became the Union's Lancashire Secretary. For twenty years he served as the Union President, a position more powerful than modern day chroniclers may suppose. From an early age he attended the major socialist events not just in the United Kingdom but also, critically for his future success, across Europe.

The life experience of the mills, the political education drawn from building the trade unions, and the friends made and trust developed even before Parliament beckoned would later save Britain from starvation, Germany from Nazism and the world from war.

The morning after the Kingsway Hall rally, Clynes called one of his weekly lunches of the 'Big Five', the undisputed power brokers and leaders of the Labour movement. Along with Clynes, the mill boy, were Henderson, Thomas, MacDonald and Snowden. This truly was a working-class shadow Cabinet of giants: Henderson, deeply religious, had started work in the iron foundry, and had refused promotion to foreman to take up his trade union position; Thomas was a railwayman who came to leadership through his analytical brain and his understanding of the use of power; Snowden, the financial genius, heavy smoking, workaholic who bettered Churchill in the chamber and finally MacDonald, orator supreme who more than any of them could sway the intelligentsia.

The strategy they thrashed out, or rather honed down, (Clynes had been pursuing it since 1906) had three pillars. First was to continue the gradualist approach that had so far delivered success. The British Labour Party needed to maximise the Labour vote *and* attract those who did not perceive themselves to have a self interest in voting Labour. Clynes knew from bitter experience in Oldham that even the working class could not be relied upon to vote blindly for Labour. They had to be convinced. The difference between Clynes and his detractors was that he welcomed this. The Socialist who took a class vote for granted very quickly ceased to be a democrat.

In his memoirs, written in 1937 after his premiership ended, he described his feelings towards the electorate. Labour people in the early years, he says, were seen as 'cranks'. So their second task was to make a psychological breakthrough, establishing the idea that a working-class man, let alone woman, was fit to govern. He was one of a handful who, through participation in Lloyd George's First World War coalition, had shown that they could govern, and, in Clynes's case, govern very well. Indeed he had been one of the first three Labour Party members to hold ministerial office.

As Minister for Food Rationing, many believed he had saved the country from starvation. The outcome of the First World War was a race between Germany's naval blockade of Britain, strangling supplies, and Britain's military conquest of a Germany who was herself starving to death. Clynes's organisational skills, honed as a trade unionist, and his commanding of a communications strategy in mobilising the best instinct of the British for fair shares, had been remarkable. And the public knew it. Here was a mill boy who now sat at the highest tables in the land – and had got there in style.

If leftists and revolutionaries said that he was carrying out the capitalists' bidding, his response was that it was his people who would have starved without his efforts and he was damned if he was leaving the job to a Tory.

Third, if Labour was ever to convince the electorate to carry Clynes to No. 10, it had to disprove the potent right-wing charge that it was an atheist and pro-Communist party, and smother the threat of Clynes's old enemy in the unions. Whatever the working class demanded in Britain, Bolshevism it was not. The fear that Labour was merely a Trojan horse for Communist domination was ever present. Worse, Labour was handicapped by its pacifist history. Fortunately, Clynes's anti-Communist credentials were to benefit his party and his country to an extent that even he, who had come so far, could not dream.

Yet early in the new parliament the issue that dominated Clynes's leadership and secured his place in the history books was not the threat of Communism but Germany's war reparation payments.

In January 1923 Germany's humiliation was pressed home by the French. Clynes watched helplessly as Ruhr coal, in payment enforced by the Treaty of Versailles, flooded the British market and depressed the price of British coal and, with it, miners' wages. In his view Versailles was a disaster. It was fuelling Bolshevism in Britain and nationalism in Germany. So when French troops marched into the Ruhr to enforce Versailles, Clynes, as Leader of the Opposition, decided to act. The ensuing socialist conference of European countries in March that year was critical in mapping out an alternative strategy to that of Paris and London, based on international- ism and the enforcement of League of Nations decisions. His key ally at that conference was his German comrade from the German Socialist Democratic Party, Herr Otto Wells.

Perhaps only such a renowned anti-Communist could approach the issue of British–Soviet relations. His shadow Foreign Secretary, MacDonald, was not trusted given his pacifist background, his opting out of the Great War and his dalliances with metropolitan Communist sympathisers and pro-Communist members of the PLP.

So Clynes had a tightrope to walk: pursue moderate poli- cies within the Labour Party to bring the public with him, but simultaneously challenge the foreign policy orthodoxy of the Entente Cordiale and widen Britain's European friendships beyond the Élysée and as far as the Kremlin.

As the year wore on, Clynes's position strengthened. The Conservatives were weary, the Liberals hopelessly divided and Labour were sounding more and more like the party of gov- ernment. His inclusive style suited the broad church of Labour in Parliament. His track record and undoubted commitment kept the trade unions on board. What he lacked in (appar- ent) flair was made up by those around him. Whenever the Fabians and intellectuals flinched, he despatched MacDonald to charm or Snowden to persuade, to keep their eye on the prize.

His secret weapon, though, was Margaret, his wife of twenty years and mother of his two sons and one daughter. Known to the close family as Polly, she was loyal, intelligent, steadfast and the ultimate political animal. She organised him, held him together and gave him the confidence that could have come from a childhood on the shop floor of the area known throughout the world as 'King Cotton' – Lancashire.

With a weak minority government, an election was inevitable. It came in December 1922. By then, Clynes enjoyed the strongest platform of any Labour leader to date. And he played his cards with his usual quiet confidence.

Before heading back to Manchester to launch his own campaign (which he did by kicking off a football match at Manchester United), he paid a last-minute visit to the family home in Putney. He discussed the future with Polly and they resolved that whatever happened they would keep their beloved home. They did, though, make a few preparations, just in case the Palace called and they had to move to Downing Street.

The Labour Party did not win the election outright but the Tory Party lost it. Clynes's troops swelled to 211, Labour's largest to date. The Conservatives lost 108 MPs (down 347 to 239) and, with them, the moral authority to govern.

On 17 January 1924, Clynes moved the motion of no confidence in Baldwin's wounded and battered government.

The debate took three days. His centrepiece was not the conditions in the factories or mines or the lack of education and health care for the common man. Rather it was the issue that rattled the Tories and terrified the country and the wider world: foreign policy.

The subsequent King's speech opened with the pledge that the government would maintain good relationships with foreign countries. Clynes went for the jugular:

'My relations with foreign powers continue to be friendly.' Is that accurate? I allege that it is not! And if we are not careful about anything else which appears in the speech from the Throne, we ought to be careful about facts. What is the position

with respect to Russia? Russia is a great foreign power. Are our
relations friendly with that foreign power? If we are on terms of
friendship with Russia, how is it that we have not received her
representatives, as we long ago properly received the representatives of Germany? Is it because Russia has not undertaken to pay
her debts? If this is a bar to recognition, how is it that we have
representatives of France here?

Labour saw clearly that the foreign policy of the Liberals and
Tories was locked in the past. In Clynes's view, the vindictive
and greedy terms of the Versailles Treaty had left Europe like an
armed camp riddled by dissension and vengeful rage. Post-war
interference and muddle, and the rise of hot-headed dictators,
had made things steadily worse up to 1924.

His olive branch towards Moscow was not to be seen as a
move towards Communism. Rather, the conventional wisdom
of allying Britain so closely with France to the exclusion of all
other countries was, in his mind, economic and political folly.
Less than six years had passed since the Great War and while
patriotism was near its high water mark, the fear of another
war was the dominant factor in the minds of the British
people. Provoking enmity with foreign powers, whatever their
ideological persuasion or outlook, did not fit with the times.
The House agreed and the motion was passed.

There is nothing in political life as tense as a crucial vote
in the House of Commons. 'Ayes to the right, three hundred
and forty-eight, Nos to the left, two hundred and thirty-
six' called out Speaker Whitley. Even at his point of victory,
Clynes remained calm and in control. As the order papers
fluttered and backs were slapped in eager congratulations,
Clynes ordered his whips to quell the nascent humming of the
socialist anthem, 'the Red flag'. He knew what the right-wing

populist, John Bull, would make of that. And in any event, it was foolishly premature; the vote had been won with over 100 Liberal votes, none of whom clamoured for the nationalisation of the British economy.

And so it was that on the 20 January 1924, before the Labour Party had reached the age of majority, King George V summoned the first Labour Prime Minister to Buckingham Palace.

In fact, he summoned the 'Big Five' to receive their seals of office. He wanted them to know that he recognised and accepted them as the legitimate government and that their lowly backgrounds did not affect his judgement. Indeed he went out of his way to wish them luck. The King was asked later how he took to welcoming the first government to come from the working classes: 'My grandfather would have hated it, my father would have tolerated it but I march with the times.'

The relationship between this monarch and his First Minister was among the strongest in the country's history. George V quickly developed a deep respect for his new Prime Minister, whose life journey he held in awe, and he learned much about his realm. It would be foolish to say that the King welcomed a socialist government but his commitment to the British system was profound. The respect was reciprocated by Clynes who famously said that as long as the monarch recognised the sovereignty of Parliament, he had nothing to fear from an organised Labour Party. Writing in tribute to his King, Clynes noted, 'King George remains at Buckingham Palace because he is a democrat ... The history of the past thirty years affords many instances of rulers whose thrones have been overturned because they set themselves stubbornly to defend the "divine rights" claimed by royalties in a previous century.'

Indeed, within the year, George V was to save British democracy.

The early days of the new government went well. Labour were fresh and focused, and expectations were high (though that was more for the country than the government). Any worries about Labour's fitness to govern were soon dispelled as the economy grew and a clear strategy emerged. The Liberals sat on their hands so the government was, by the standards of the day, stable. Apart from the sneering press over the trivial issue of whether the Cabinet should wear morning and dress suits, there was no sight of the predicted calamity of a socialist upheaval. (Clynes hated wearing the 'establishments' garbs but Polly said he had no choice, he was Prime Minister after all. So that was an end to the matter.)

The Cabinet proposals on housing, welfare and education got support from Labour and Liberal backbenchers alike. More difficult was disarmament, but here Clynes and Snowden, his Chancellor, started the long painful process of turning round the Versailles process. In a series of secret bi-laterals held in neutral Geneva, Clynes and his old friend Otto Wells mapped out a mutually beneficial path.

Alongside the disarmament talks, the rescheduling and pruning of Germany's reparation payments was made palatable by bringing Russia into the picture – trade opportunities helped fuel the growth that both Britain and Germany needed.

The Tory backbenchers, though, couldn't swallow it. The idea of the working classes governing Britain offended their sense of what was fitting. They had been brought up to rule and many of them had foregone a fortune in the Square Mile and in industry to serve the public. When Clynes's disarmament programmes stared to affect the share values of their engineering companies, then 'something had to be done'.

It was no surprise that the 'someone' who took it upon himself to do the something was the Member for Epping Forest and shadow Chancellor of the Exchequer, Winston Churchill. He could barely bring himself to tolerate his own front bench with their naive Francophile view of the world, but to have that 'Little Piecer' upstart from Oldham in 10 Downing Street was enough to burst his blood vessels.

Churchill had tried before to halt Clynes's political career.

In the very early days of Labour a common goal was to have working-class people appointed as local magistrates. Partly this was because hungry youngsters were being given severe sentences for nothing more than stealing to feed their families. Partly it was a political strategy – the appointment into a public position helped build the trade unions' and Labour's credibility. One such nominee in Oldham in 1901 was Clynes.

His appointment was blocked by his own MP. On 18 April 1901, Churchill wrote to his father's friend, Lord James of Hereford, then a Cabinet member, asking him to intervene. In a letter written in Churchill's own hand, he stated:

> Mr Clynes is not v[er]y satisfactory and his appointment would cause dissatisfaction on the conservative side in Oldham, as he is reputed to be a v[er]y active partisan of the Radical party.

Lord James did his bidding and Clynes, although he didn't know the precise reason why, was turned down.

Now Churchill was playing for much higher stakes and he knew where Labour's Achilles' heel lay: the Red under the Bed.

Throughout the spring and summer of 1924, Herbert Asquith and Stanley Baldwin grew increasingly nervous. Asquith saw that his own party was facing annihilation as Labour took the mantle of progressive politics and Baldwin realised the popularity of what Labour was doing. The unemployment benefit improvements, the creation of a national electricity grid, a road building programme and a boost to social housing under the Wheatley Act were all both pragmatic and attractive to the public. Alongside this, disarmament was easing the debt and Germany's sabre rattling was soothed by Labour's international success. MacDonald spent most of the time in Geneva and, with Clynes and Snowden's backing, Europe was looking towards trade-driven prosperity not arms-driven war-mongering.

In the midst of this, as a latter day statesman would have said, there came 'an event'.

Few people outside of the Communist newspaper *Workers' Weekly* had heard of Mr John Campbell, its acting editor. However, an article in late July had caused concern in the War Office. Ironically it was a Labour Parliamentary Secretary, in the reading room at the Liberal Club on Horse Guards parade, who spotted the offending piece. The Admiralty Minister, Charles Ammon MP, was researching a speech when he happened upon a small editorial which exhorted soldiers 'to let it be known that neither in the class war nor in military war will you turn your guns on your fellow workers'.

Ammon was a good man. A local councillor in Camberwell and General Secretary of the Dock Workers' Union, he didn't know much about the Navy but he knew a lot about ships and sailors. What he read stunned him. Without contacting the whips' office or No. 10, but out of the best of motives, he telephoned Sir Patrick Hastings, the Attorney-General.

Hastings, one of Britain's most successful lawyers, was already on the case. The Director of Public Prosecutions had referred the article to him. Now, with direct contact from the Admiralty, Hasting acted. On 6 August Campbell's house was raided by Scotland Yard and he was arrested.

Predictably, it was James Maxton MP who kicked up a fuss in Campbell's defence, warning the Attorney-General that the Labour MPs would defend the Communist editor. Hastings wavered and sought an audience with the Prime Minister. Clynes would not budge. He would not countenance withdrawing the prosecution. To give the impression of going soft on Communism would not only be wrong but political suicide.

Campbell eventually served six months in prison for incitement to mutiny. By then, what turned out to be a small affair had been buried by the dirtiest political trick in modern times.

Asquith and Lloyd George, realising that their enmity was no less than mutually assured destruction, had buried their differences, conspired with Baldwin and decided that the Labour Party was being too successful, and needed to be brought down more than a peg or two. A general election was forced upon Clynes's minority government. The election date was set for Wednesday 29 October 1924.

Watching the Campbell affair and admiring Clynes's sure footedness, despite the pressure heaped upon him, was an increasingly frustrated Churchill. He knew that the reason why the Campbell arrest had been so potent was the vulnerability of Labour to the pro-Communist charge. So Churchill set a conspiracy in motion.

Grigori Zinoviev, Head of the Communist International in Moscow, was one of the most powerful men in the world. If anyone was to be the conduit for a Soviet-inspired insurrection in Britain, it would be he. If a letter purportedly from Zinoviev to the British Communist Party were to fall into the hands of the Foreign Office, and simultaneously be given kudos by the intelligence service and perchance fall into the hands of the *Daily Mail*, then the election might well swing away from Labour.

This was the scheme hatched by Churchill.

By chance, Clynes was staying overnight in Huddersfield with Snowden, having finished a punishing day of election rallies across Yorkshire. He was due in his own constituency the following morning of Saturday 25 October. Clynes and Snowden were as close as any Prime Minister and Chancellor could be. The former knew that the latter didn't want his job. The Chancellor for his part knew that whatever his command of economics, his boss had the better political brain. Between them they bestrode Labour politics.

Before turning in, they were discussing the election outcome and whether to ramp up the German–British disarmament programme when the telephone rang. It was No. 10. They had on the line the duty press officer. Tomorrow's *Daily Mail* was carrying a front page headline: 'Civil War plot by Socialists'. The forged Zinoviev letter was out there.

Fleet Street was thrown into frenzy and the Labour Party went into meltdown.

The sign of true leadership is to remain calm in the face of a crisis. Clynes instinctively knew the letter was a forgery and, if he didn't know where it had originated, he could hazard a guess. He also knew that the future of the Labour movement rested on his shoulders and with it the chances of peace in Europe.

He calculated that public trust in his personal anti-Communist credentials (so much better established than that of some of his prominent colleagues, including his Foreign Secretary and his party) would be critical. He felt on strong ground and so he turned to the staunchest defender of British parliamentary democracy he knew – King George V.

The two men had already discussed the issue of Soviet–British relations at great length. The King had only half jokingly asked his Prime Minister to do what he had to do with the Soviet Union, but to refrain from shaking hands with the people who had murdered his cousins. As trust between the two had grown, George had accepted that Clynes's objection to Communism was based on a real fear that a workers' revolution would lead to bloodshed and hardship not for the rich but for the very workers who Bolshevism claimed to speak for. The King suspected that the *Daily Mail* was involved in a conspiracy and that whatever some in the Labour ranks privately desired, his government was patriotic, as were the millions who voted for it.

The following morning, as the political fall-out from the *Mail* scoop exploded over the general election campaign, Clynes travelled home to Manchester.

The Midland Hotel, Manchester was most renowned as the place where a Mr Rolls and a Mr Royce, twenty years previously, had met and agreed to form a motor company. It was now the venue for a telephone call that would change the course of history. The Prime Minister telephoned his King.

Among the other attributes that separated Clynes from his challenger MacDonald was his ability to negotiate. Whereas MacDonald would schmooze and hypothecate, Clynes would start with his toughest opening bid: 'Did the King trust the patriotism of his Prime Minister and, if he did, what was he prepared to do to defend it?'

George V's predecessors would have stayed well out of the matter. But the current monarch calculated that if the working class believed that the election was stolen from them, they could lose faith with the democratic system with disastrous consequences. He had to do the right thing.

Private secretaries are called upon to carry out many tasks. Some seem trivial, while some are of obvious importance. The good private secretary carries out both such tasks with equal professionalism because he knows that sometimes the small task carries a huge implication. Sometimes he quietly and mildly urges caution and other times he knows when to do as told. The best private secretary in Britain was the King's, Lieutenant Colonel, the Right Honourable Lord Stamfordham, formerly Arthur Bigge.

When George V called Arthur that morning with a delicate ring of the silver bell and instructed him to summon the editor of the London *Daily Mail* to the Palace, he knew better than to interfere.

The following day, the affair was forgotten. A small article appeared on page five of the *Mail* saying that an investigation was being undertaken by the Manchester police force into an apparently forged letter, purporting to be from a Mr Zinoviev. It was made clear that there was cross-party consensus that the matter should be cleared up so as to avoid any chance of damaging Britain's relations with foreign powers. The suggestion in some quarters that the official opposition were involved was categorically denied by a No. 10 press officer 'speaking with the authority of the Prime Minister'.

Clynes's committee rooms for the October 1924 election were in the premises of the Popular Picture Theatre in Miles Platting. As the results started to come in Clynes's supporters suppressed their excitement. It was eighteen years since they had first elected the quietly-spoken son of an Irish immigrant as their Member of Parliament.

In the hours waiting for his own result the theatre was packed to the doors and a silent crowd, many thousands strong, filled the streets outside. Conflicting rumours sent them alternately into despair and delight, but when it was ascertained that he had won, and he arrived by car, the cheering masses were packed so densely that he had to be carried over their heads in a chair, or he would have never got into the theatre at all. For ten minutes after he arrived, he could not get a hearing, and when he did speak less than a score or so could hear what he said.

By the early hours, the only remaining question was whether Labour would have an outright majority or be beholden to a handful of Lloyd George's Liberals. The situation was entirely new to British politics. The divisions among the Liberals were pretty much put to bed as Asquith had lost his seat in what was a near wipe-out for the party that had governed for so long. Labour's hour had arrived and its hero was the mill boy who had started his working life at the tender age of ten years old.

The final tally showed Labour with 310 Members of Parliament and the rump of the Liberals holding the balance of power with fewer than fifty seats. There was no question of the Liberals propping up a Tory government; Lloyd George, whatever else he was, was a radical.

For many years he and his party had argued for a new electoral system of proportional representation. Clynes had some sympathy with the view that the existing system did cause dislocation. With four million votes, the Liberals on a proportional system would have carried around 110 seats.

On the other side of the argument was the compelling warning from Germany: tiny parties wielding disproportionate power. The Prime Minister had always been more attracted to a version of the Alternative Vote in which votes were cast for single-member seats with the second preferences of the third placed candidate transferred first. This was the system used by the trade unions, and had brought fairness and stability there. There were some advantages to the Liberals as well, especially in seats where neither of the big two parties were likely to win outright. Most important, it locked in an anti-laissez faire majority. If the two could strike a deal, never again would the power of Parliament be used to starve Britons into submission, as it had been during the general strike.

Clynes was not a personal friend of David Lloyd George, much as he admired his talents. Indeed, unlike MacDonald and, to a lesser extent, Snowden, Clynes, Henderson and Thomas were not part of the socialite circles of the West End. It wasn't that he didn't feel comfortable with the elite, indeed his relationship with George V was the envy of Baldwin and much of the Tory front bench. Rather, he didn't feel it mattered. In the world he came from, whether or not he was invited to Lady Birkenhead's parties was a matter of complete indifference.

In real politics this was a weakness in the Prime Minister and something Sidney and Beatrice Webb worried over. Labour may be able to maintain the parliamentary arithmetic without the movers and shakers of the London social scene but they made the chemistry of government very difficult for themselves. It was to the Webbs that Clynes turned to as conduits when he needed to cut a deal with Lloyd George.

Hampstead, north London, is the geographical home of the progressive intelligentsia. For over twenty-five years, the Webbs had lived at 10 Netherhall Gardens, just off the Finchley Road behind Swiss Cottage. It was here, on the evening of Sunday 2 November 1924, that the method of electing the British Parliament was determined for the next hundred years.

The 1925 Electoral Representation Act stood the test of time. It introduced Universal Suffrage for all people aged twenty-one years and over on the basis of the Alternative Vote in a single-member constituency. Even Lloyd George saw the advantage of Clynes's argument about third place candidates transferring their votes first.

The next morning, Buckingham Palace phoned the Clynes family home in Putney, where Polly and Jack had stayed the night, rather than at No. 10. It was Beatrice Webb's suggestion that they stayed at home so as not to appear presumptuous. Sidney had argued otherwise; he wanted Clynes to stay over in Hampstead so the call came there.

As Clynes accepted the seals of office again, he discussed the make-up of the new Cabinet with the King. Only one of the 'Big Five' could not carry on: MacDonald was exhausted. His eyesight had also started to cause real concern and it was felt that it would be kinder to give him a less onerous position than that of Foreign Secretary.

This caused a problem. Foreign affairs, in particular the treaty with Russia, and the rising resentment against the French in Germany as Versailles still took its political toll, were, the King and Prime Minister agreed, the priority. Henderson, Thomas and Snowden could cope with the domestic front, where the prospect of strike action in the key industries had diminished with Labour's return to office and the improved price of coal.

It was the King's suggestion in the end. George V had a greater intimacy with foreign, especially European affairs, than any monarch before, and possibly since. He understood better than most the disturbing potential of Germany. So why, he asked, didn't the Prime Minister combine the two jobs: PM and Foreign Secretary?

The problem in Europe, they both understood from their different perspectives, was not just the revolutionary nature of Russia or the hurt pride of France but rather the instability of the Weimar Republic. Democracy in Germany was a new idea and it wasn't working.

Although the imposition of Versailles was commonly seen as the problem, Clynes, influenced by his dear friend Otto

Wells, knew the problem went deeper than that. In November 1918, as far as the German army and much of public opinion were concerned, Germany hadn't lost the war but had given in. And it was the new left-wing democratic politicians who had capitulated in November 1918 on the day of the so called 'stab in the back'. Many felt that democracy was the cause of, not the solution to, Germany's woes and its resulting weakness in standing up for itself.

Worse, the proportional representation system of the Weimar Republic with its unaccountable list system was creating not a healthy democracy but chaos. By 1925 there were over two dozen parties represented in the Reichstag and decision making was all but impossible. Worse, many of the smaller parties saw a common scapegoat for Germany's problems. The so called November plotters who had surrendered Germany's prestige included a number of Jews.

So with political instability, economic meltdown, foreign troops on her soil, territory lost to enemies – and all because some back-stabbing politician had betrayed the Fatherland – Germany was on its knees.

On the home front, with the guarantees from Lloyd George's Liberals in return for the Alternative Vote Act, Labour now entered a period of stable government. The programmes of social housing, introduced earlier by the Wheatley Act, were expanded. As a result millions of people moved from their derelict terraced houses with outside toilets into warm, heated homes. Coal, steel and railways provided the pillars of a growing British economy based not on re-armament but shared prosperity. Trade with Russia and America grew. Fears of a Socialist debacle diminished and Labour, although on probation, gained general approval.

But Clynes was focused on the increasing problem

in Europe. His understanding of German hurt eased the situation and his suggestion to Wells that a campaign for a referendum in Sudetenland gained support in Prague as well as Berlin. The reparations issue continued to cause problems between France and Germany, but with Britain, and the trade and commerce that came through its Commonwealth, providing the engine of the European economy, the problem was simmering not boiling.

Yet the economic storm that was about to break did not brew in Berlin or Moscow, much less London, but in New York.

Central to the 1924–29 Labour government strategy was the development of the League of Nations. The experience of the Great War seared into the minds of the government. It was the British working class who had paid the price in the loss of their young men.

The Treaty of Versailles had specified that 'Germany should disarm so as to open the way to universal disarmament'. The choice facing the Western powers was not, as the Conservative benches debated, between re-arming to quell the potential threat of an arms race with Germany on the one hand or an accommodation with the German public's ambition on the other. It was, as the King's speech in November 1925 insisted, the development of a League of Nations that the old world and the new world could and would enforce. The surest way in the late 1920s of prompting re-armament in Germany was for Britain to do just that.

A pre-requisite for peace and prosperity, therefore, was a Germany at ease with itself. The Labour government understood this.

Clynes, like the majority of the Labour movement, had opposed the war. He understood it as a capitalist war that would benefit the industrialists' profits and starve, maim and kill his people. Yet once the course was set, he had no hesitation but to put his shoulder to the wheel of the national effort. At the end of hostilities, he had argued that Labour should remain in the coalition but he was out-voted by the special Labour conference. As ever, putting loyalty before self, he had resigned forthwith from Lloyd George's unity government. He achieved the double objective of showing Labour could govern and maintaining unity in the Movement.

His experience as Minister of Food Rationing had given him an intimate understanding of the British and German economy. The war was not just fought by the armies and navies of the two powers but by the public's willingness to support that effort.

The electorate trusted Clynes more than it had trusted any other politician before. He understood how the need to invest in economies, combined with a nationalist fervour, could result in a call to arms which would render another war more, not less, likely. 'Mars grows lusty under our tender nurturing of him. The God of War is the cuckoo in our national nest' he wrote. The world was therefore fortunate that the British Prime Minister was not, peace loving though he was, an idealist.

He also understood how to negotiate. Years of bargaining, cajoling and persuading bloody-minded employers and suspicious trade union members had taught him a lot about human nature. He knew that there were two types of mandates, one to compromise and one with red lines. A representative who crossed the red lines would soon no longer be a representative. At fifty-five, he had learned that this was the weakness and the strength of a democratic system. He understood that this was the case with Weimar Republic.

Yet however much he laboured in Lausanne and Geneva at the reparation and disarmament talks, the German debt that had been built up *since* 1918 was still owed to Wall Street, irrespective of how Britain unpicked Versailles.

When Labour were re-elected on 30 May 1929, this time with an overall working majority, Britain's economy was strong. Clynes was at the height of his powers. His eldest son William had left home bound for Madagascar with an ambition to own a tobacco plantation. His daughter May had married, but the younger son had still not settled down.

So as Parliament rose on 26 July 1929 for a long deserved recess, Labour had been in power, more or less successfully, for six years and John Robert Clynes headed up a post-war Britain looking confidently at the world.

It fell to Jimmy Thomas, former railwayman and now Lord Privy Seal, to open the new Parliament on 29 October that year. He was respected by Parliament and indeed loved by many of his own side. Despite twenty-three years in Parliament, six years of them in high office, he was still teased by his colleagues for dropping his 'h's. The sketch-writers' favourite was when he told the House he had 'a 'ell of an 'eadache'. As he rose to the despatch box at 2.45 p.m. to face oral questions on employment matters, he waited anxiously for messages from the civil service box giving news from New York. There, it was 9.45 a.m.

All week the Dow Jones index had been falling. That day it was falling fast. Richard Whitney, Vice Chairman of the Dow, had been instructed the previous Thursday by the heads of the banks to shore up stocks and shares to keep confidence in the United States economy. Now it was clear that the tactic wasn't working. By the time the House of Commons rose that evening in London, $30 billion had been wiped off the share values in New York in less than a week.

The repercussions in Britain were bad enough. The next day the Ebbw Vale mine went into insolvency and unemployment

threatened again. In Germany, economics once again moved
centre stage.

No amount of politics could take away the fact that
Germany's economy had been financed by American money.
This was on top of the £6,600 million pounds owed to France
and Belgium.

As the Cabinet met in emergency session that Sunday,
Clynes made sure that their policy response was not just
domestic. By the late 1920s the economy was global and inter-
dependent. Protectionism, tariffs and re-armament were the
populist calls of the day from the opposition benches and some
of his own on the left and the right. Now was the time, he told
his Cabinet, to lift their horizons, to strengthen the League of
Nations and to use their Commonwealth to the benefit of all.

His colleagues did not know about his conversations with
Otto Wells. In Germany, revolution was stirring. A combination of political instability and the economic crisis were
driving voters to the extremes. Between them the German
National Socialist Workers party and the Communist Party
were touching 30 per cent of popular support in the opinion
polls. Wells pleaded with Clynes to help and not to abandon
democracy in Germany. He felt sure the policies of France, and
the Conservatives of all persuasions in Britain, would isolate
Germany and plunge it into civil unrest at best and, at worst, a
revolution against democracy.

The Cabinet was asked in very gentle, persuasive, cautionary
and chillingly logical fashion to renounce Versailles and enter
into negotiations for a European economic order in return
for a new constitution based on a remodelled voting system
in Germany. The fear of Bolshevism motivated some such as
Henderson and Thomas. The fear of depression motivated the
Chancellor, Snowden, who backed his Prime Minister by laying

out the necessity for a global response using arguments from respected economists such as his dear friend John Maynard Keynes. For some, Sidney Webb included, an understanding of what anti-semitism could do to humanity was decisive.

For all of them their loyalty and trust in Clynes, for who he was, as well as what he had done, meant they would give him their support in any event.

There was no vote in the Cabinet. The Commons did divide but with a strong Labour majority passed its support for the emergency package. On hearing the news, a cheer went up in the Reichstag. One man did not celebrate. The leader of the National Socialists, Herr Hitler, left the chamber a defeated man.

John Robert Clynes died in Putney on 23 October 1949 three weeks after the death of his wife Polly. He was the last survivor of the 1906 intake. His successor as Labour leader and Prime Minister, Clement Attlee MP, told the House of Commons that democracy had lost 'its greatest proponent'.

Today there is no Clynes College at Oxford or Cambridge. There is a John Clynes Crescent in Miles Platting just off the Oldham Road and there is a Clynes Close in Putney on the site of his former home. History is not kind to those who do not write it.

Prime Minister Halifax attempts peace with Hitler

Hugh Purcell

Deep in the Yorkshire Wolds outside the village of Kirby Underdale stands the family church of the Earls of Halifax. Inside is a plaque to commemorate a long forgotten event, the Conversations of Malines (1921–25), in which Viscount Halifax strove with Cardinal Mercier for 'the Reunification of Christendom'. There they are in a stained glass window kneeling either side of God, out of whose mouth come the words 'That they all may be one'. His son, later the First Earl of Halifax who became Prime Minister in 1940, resembled his father in high Anglican beliefs and in a love of country pursuits, which is why Winston Churchill called him 'the Holy Fox'.

Like his father, too, Lord Halifax was by nature a man of compromise and like his father he failed. For it was his disastrous attempt to placate Hitler in 1940 and seek a compromise peace between the British Empire and Nazi Germany that led to his fall from office – the shortest serving Prime Minister in British history.

Of all the Prime Ministers-in-waiting of the twentieth century, none had such a golden opportunity of succeeding as Lord Halifax. The crucial meeting to decide who should succeed Neville Chamberlain took place in the Cabinet room at 4.30 p.m. on 9 May 1940. Present were the abdicating Prime

Minister and the two senior ministers contending to succeed him, Lord Halifax, Foreign Secretary, and Winston Churchill, First Lord of the Admiralty and member of the War Cabinet. Also present was David Margesson, the Conservative Chief Whip. Halifax must have entered the room knowing that the top job in British politics was his for the taking. He was the choice of King George VI, Chamberlain himself and, according to Margesson, the majority of the House of Commons, including the Labour Party that had precipitated the crisis by refusing to serve in a national government under Chamberlain.

* * *

On 4 April 1940, Prime Minister Neville Chamberlain announced complacently that Hitler 'had missed the bus' by not invading Western Europe. Five days later the Nazis invaded Denmark and Norway and swept all before them, including units of the British Army, which were forced to withdraw ignominiously, and the Navy, which failed to engage. This brought to a head increasing widespread dissatisfaction with the Prime Minister's lacklustre conduct of the war. A Commons debate on 7 and 8 May turned into a vote of no confidence in Chamberlain. The government won the debate technically, but over forty Tory backbenchers voted with the opposition and many more abstained. Chamberlain had to go. The rebels from all sides agreed that a national coalition government was the only answer.

Why, then, was Lord Halifax the preferred choice to lead it? Fifty-nine years of age, tall and gaunt, rational but manipulative ('foxy' again), he had served as a reforming Viceroy of India (as Lord Irwin, 1926–31) and then became an exponent of appeasement. In the 1930s 'appeasement' was not a pejorative word. It implied taking the moral high ground, standing for idealism, magnanimity and the willingness to right wrongs; a generous pragmatism, even a hallmark of liberal conservatism. Perhaps for this reason, Halifax totally misjudged Hitler when he first met him in 1937 and for some time afterwards. He even compared him to Gandhi. 'Nationalism and Racialism is a powerful force but I can't feel that it's either unnatural or immoral,' he said the same year – a remark that came back to haunt him. Nevertheless, as Foreign Secretary from 1938 to 1940 he saw through Hitler before his Prime Minister did. After Chamberlain's second visit to meet Hitler over Czechoslovakia in September 1938, Halifax announced to the Cabinet the following morning that Hitler was not to be trusted; Nazism had to be eliminated. That did not stop Halifax during the 'phoney war' of 1939–40 from listening to proposals to mediate with Germany. A diplomat by nature he sought compromise, hated the emotional or rash and believed in the round-table skills of patient listening and gradual manipulation. Although he admitted that he was a 'layman' in all things military, both the House of Lords and the Commons respected him for his experience and wisdom. He was a 'favourite' of the royal family and in this constitutional crisis the King, as kings have always done, could show preferment to him.

Churchill was the opposite. He loved the clash of arms, rejoiced in being emotional, was a diehard imperialist and sometimes behaved more like a 'cad' than a gentleman. He was widely mistrusted as a man of excess, including with alcohol, whose judgement and temperament were unstable. Chamberlain had already tipped off Halifax that he wanted him as successor and although Halifax had not expressed any enthusiasm, neither had he ruled out the prospect. He told

Chamberlain that as a peer there would be difficulties sitting in the House of Lords, wary of becoming an 'honorary Prime Minister, living in a kind of twilight just outside the things that really mattered'. But Halifax had also told his Under Secretary 'Rab' Butler that he thought he could do the job and that Churchill needed restraining.

That was the thought uppermost in his mind on the afternoon of 9 May: Churchill needed restraining. He probably shared the Tory view that Churchill had made many wrong decisions in the 1920s and before, always impulsive, often reactionary – landing allied troops at Gallipoli, intervening in the Russian civil war, wanting to fight the striking unions in 1926 – but in the 1930s the contenders for the premiership in 1940 had personally clashed over two major political events. The first was Halifax's attempts as Viceroy of India to devolve power by an alliance with Gandhi which was undermined by Churchill's offensive insult that India's 'mahatma' (holy man) was nothing better than 'a seditious lawyer… posing as a fakir and striding half-naked up the steps of the Viceregal palace'. The second was the abdication of Edward VIII when Halifax took the moral high ground of his family that remarriage after divorce was still bigamy, while Churchill, in his romantic, monarchical way, supported the reigning King.

Halifax was not a man to bear grudges. In his cool but calculating way he was a man of political judgement who deplored the misjudgements of others. Since the start of the war in 1939 it seemed that Churchill had made few decisions that were not misjudgements. He had wanted to take military action against Eire (October 1939) and then in defence of Finland (November 1939); he had made a disastrous broadcast in January 1940, in which he had described neutral countries as burying their heads in the sand hoping that the

German crocodile would eat their neighbours first; and then, in April and May, he had been responsible operationally for the Norwegian fiasco. Stanley Baldwin had said of Churchill years before that he lacked 'judgement and wisdom. And that is why while we delight to listen to him in the House we do not take his advice.' The Tory party agreed with that view.

Unlike some of his colleagues, Halifax was not in awe of Churchill. He did not relish confrontation but he did have a strong sense of patriotic duty. Moreover, he was not a Tory loyalist and he welcomed the present necessity for a national government. For all these reasons, when Chamberlain told the assembled quartet that he had decided to resign and turned to Halifax first as the senior minister present, Halifax accepted the premiership. Churchill offered his loyal support.

Lord Halifax 'kissed hands' with a grateful King on the evening of 9 May and straight away an enabling Bill was passed allowing him to sit and speak in the Commons without renouncing his title. He took the unprecedented step of retaining his post as Foreign Secretary for the duration of the crisis.

As often happens at a time of crisis, the British people were surprisingly calm that month. Mass Observation summarised the national mood as late as 24 May under the heading 'Morale Today': 'There is a slight increase in anxiety and a slight decrease in optimism. There is a general recognition of the seriousness of the situation, but still little idea that this could be more than a temporary setback.' Lord Halifax and the rest of the War Cabinet had no such illusions. On 15 May the Prime Minister asked Churchill to employ his rhetorical skills and international reputation to write to President Roosevelt, aware that France might surrender and urgently wanting to bring America into the war:

As you are no doubt aware, the scene has darkened swiftly. If necessary we shall continue the war alone and we are not afraid of that. But I trust you realise, Mr President that the voice and the force of the United States may count for nothing if you withhold too long. You may have a completely subjugated, Nazified Europe established with astonishing swiftness, and the weight may be more than we can bear.

Roosevelt trusted neither Britain's intention to resist nor, under Halifax, its determination to go it alone. On 24 May he told the Prime Minister of Canada, Mackenzie King, that in case not only France but also Britain were forced to surrender, the British fleet should leave for Canada as soon as possible to escape surrender terms. That same day the British Army in France began to withdraw to the Channel ports and the next day the French Comité de Guerre considered asking Germany for peace, whether or not Britain agreed. Prime Minister Halifax regarded this with the utmost gravity. He had told the Cabinet some time before that he did not think Britain could keep fighting if France surrendered. Now his intention was to explore any diplomatic initiative that might lead to an armistice.

On Saturday 25 May, Lord Halifax asked the Italian ambassador, Guiseppe Bastianini, to meet him in the afternoon. He had heard through Italian diplomatic channels that 'if His Majesty's government saw their way to make their approach to the Italian government, with a view to exploring the possibilities of a friendly settlement, there need be no fear of their meeting with a rebuff'. The next day Prime Minister Halifax showed the War Cabinet his 'Suggested Approach to Signor Mussolini'. It read:

If Signor Mussolini will co-operate with us in securing a settlement of all European questions which safeguard the independence and the security of the allies, and could be the basis of a just and durable peace for Europe, we will undertake at once to discuss, with the desire to find solutions, the matters in which Signor Mussolini is primarily interested.

This was coupled with the text of a joint British–French appeal to Washington asking Roosevelt to inform Mussolini of the French and British willingness to consider certain Italian claims, 'to be dependent of course on Italy not entering the war against the allies'. What Halifax had in mind was the possibility of surrendering Malta, Gibraltar, Suez and some African colonies to appease the Italian appetite for control of the Mediterranean. In Halifax's mind, these dispensable outposts of Empire were a bait to persuade Mussolini to chair a sort of reconvened Versailles conference with Hitler sitting at the table. This would discuss, as Halifax put it blandly, 'the terms of a general settlement'.

It was certainly not in Halifax's mind to surrender to Hitler. All through his deliberations with the War Cabinet he spoke of maintaining the essential 'independence and liberty of our own Empire'. But he believed in the realpolitik of a balance of power. This amounted to the de jure recognition of Germany's control of central Europe in return for Hitler agreeing a truce with France and Britain. Unlike Churchill, who thought in apocalyptic terms of fighting to the finish, the Prime Minister's view was that Hitler had only won round one in a decade-long struggle and the priority now was to achieve a breathing space to get the British Army back from the Continent and save at least part of France. His underlying hopes were that Roosevelt might warn off the Fascist powers, that the German home front was shaky because of the British blockade and that Mussolini did not want Hitler as 'top dog' in Europe. All these hopes proved wrong. Yet his determination was such that he confided to his diary that 'Winston talked the most frightful rot' in opposing any approach to Italy and on Monday 27 May, Halifax went so far as to threaten his pugnacious First Lord of the Admiralty that his Prime Minister might resign if the peace process was not begun.

The next afternoon the full Cabinet assembled for the first time in several days. News of the surrender of Belgium had come in and it looked as if there was no escape from Dunkirk for the British Expeditionary Force. Prime Minister Halifax outlined his plans for a truce mediated through Mussolini. Churchill disagreed with a speech of defiance that made a huge impact on those present:

> It was idle to think that, if we made peace now, we should get better terms from Germany than if we fought it out. We should become a slave state. We shall go on and we shall fight it out. Better it should end, not through surrender but only when we are rolling senseless on the ground.

Halifax found this a histrionic response. He said later, 'common sense should dictate government policy, not bravery'. As he told the Cabinet, the proposal to fight on was not the point at issue. He wished to fight on too but open channels for negotiation at the same time. When the War Cabinet met again that evening Halifax knew that he would get his way for the time being, however emotional and troublesome his First Lord of the Admiralty might be.

The War Cabinet consisted of five members. Apart from Halifax and Churchill the others were Chamberlain, as leader of the Conservative Party and Lord President, and the two Labour leaders Clement Attlee and Arthur Greenwood.

The Labour members were newcomers to the Cabinet and, although Greenwood in particular spoke out against an approach to Mussolini, at this time at least they deferred to Halifax's authority. Chamberlain and Halifax were more or less on the same wavelength with Churchill the outsider. It was the Prime Minister's deep-felt belief, born of experience, training and character, that diplomacy might avoid a probable catastrophe. He was persistent and his authority in the War Cabinet overrode Churchill's objections. That Sunday afternoon he told the Italian ambassador, Guiseppe Bastianini, to convey to Signor Mussolini that His Majesty's government wanted him to initiate talks with Herr Hitler in pursuit of a European settlement.

It met with complete rejection. Prime Minister Halifax of all people should have known to consult his Ambassador to Italy, because Sir Percy Loraine warned the Foreign Office that very day that neither an offer to intercede from Roosevelt nor an invitation to chair a peace conference from Halifax would get anywhere. He was right. Two months before, when Mussolini had first anticipated that the blitzkrieg was about to begin, he had told the Council of Ministers that neutrality was not an option because Italy 'would lose prestige among the nations of the world' and also offend Germany to whom Italy was forged by the Pact of Steel. By 26 May he sensed he had the nation behind him. The opportunity of profiting from the expected collapse of the Western democracies was too strong to resist. So the offer from Roosevelt to intercede between Italy and the Allies was rebuffed. In fact, when the American ambassador to Rome tried to convey Roosevelt's letter to Mussolini he failed even to get an audience. A few days later when Halifax invited Mussolini to chair a peace conference the Prime Minister was turned down flat.

One immediate result of this humiliating rebuff was that on 1 June Roosevelt refused to contact Hitler on Britain's behalf. Halifax, supported by Chamberlain, had drafted a letter to Roosevelt encouraging him to inform Hitler that if Germany offered terms to Britain 'destructive of British independence' then this 'would encounter US resistance'. Why should Roosevelt intervene in this way when his own Ambassador to the United Kingdom, Joseph Kennedy, was endorsing the Halifax view that Britain could not fight on if France surrendered? Why risk another embarrassing snub?

The news that Prime Minister Halifax failed to persuade Mussolini to arbitrate a peace conference made little impact at the time. The papers were full of the deliverance at Dunkirk from where, by 4 June, 335,000 British and French troops were rescued against all the odds. His proposal was regarded by a relieved people as a sensible and uncommitted initiative, largely because Churchill remained loyal (as he had been to Chamberlain in the dread Norway debate of early May) and the 'appeasing' proposals discussed in the War Cabinet to sacrifice Empire territory like Malta and Gibraltar remained confidential, as indeed they were for many years afterwards.

On 17 June France surrendered. That day, one of the darkest in Britain's war, Prime Minister Halifax's Under Secretary 'Rab' Butler was walking in St James' Park where he happened to meet the Swedish ambassador. Affected by the gloom of the moment he told him that that the British government would lose no opportunity to conclude a compromise peace and that 'diehards' like Churchill would not be allowed to stand in the way. He repeated the Halifax summation: 'common sense and not bravery would dictate the British government's policy'. The Swedish minister reported this to Stockholm, where the King of Sweden would soon propose a peace deal to both Berlin and London. On 28 June Pope Pius XII offered semi-divine intervention when he wrote to Hitler proposing to mediate himself for 'a just and honourable peace'.

A peace with Britain was high on Hitler's agenda. Now that France had fallen he began to plan for an unforgiving attack on the Soviet Union, as forewarned in *Mein Kampf* (1926). But he had one nagging anxiety: the need to fight on two fronts if Britain remained in the war, an anxiety increased by his awareness of the colossal might of the United States that had already entered one World War, in 1917, to protect its European allies against Germany. Hence in the summer of 1940 Hitler's immediate aim was to get Britain out of the war, by persuasion or compulsion, and avoid America's involvement.

In the United States, the German embassy spent all its resources supporting the isolationists in their desire to keep America her own side of the Atlantic. In Britain, Halifax continued to receive peace offerings from Germany. Some of these came via a British diplomat in Switzerland, Sir David Kelly, who met with a German aristocrat in a very quiet little fish restaurant by a lake. The message was that 'the Führer did not wish to touch Britain or the British Empire; nor to ask for any reparation; his sole condition was that we should make peace and leave him a completely free hand in Europe'. Halifax had heard this before. As Foreign Secretary in August 1939 he had received an offer from Hitler 'to conclude agreements with England which would guarantee the existence of the British Empire in all circumstances as far as Germany was concerned', provided this 'large comprehensive offer' took effect 'after the solution of the German–Polish problem'.

Now Halifax told Sir David Kelly in Switzerland to show interest as a way of gaining time.

No doubt aware that Prime Minister Halifax had already persuaded his War Cabinet to take one peace initiative, Hitler made one last – public – peace offer to Britain. On 19 July, in a broadcast speech from the Reichstag later printed and dropped over the south of Britain from the air, he said:

> In this hour it is my duty before my own conscience to appeal once more to reason and common sense in Great Britain as much as elsewhere. I consider myself in the position to make this appeal since I am not the vanquished begging favours, but the victor speaking in the name of reason. I can see no reason why this war must go on.

The American journalist William Shirer witnessed the speech. He heard not the familiar rant but Hitler 'mixing superbly the full confidence of the conqueror with the humbleness that always goes down well with the masses when they know a man is on top'. Afterwards 'Hitler mingled with a good many officials and officers and not one of them had the slightest doubt that the British would accept what they really believed was a generous and even magnanimous offer from the Führer'.

That weekend, between Hitler's speech on the evening of Friday 19 July and Halifax's reply broadcast live on the evening of Monday 22 July, the British Prime Minister was confronted with the toughest decisions any leader can make – was it to be peace or continuing war? How could he predict the outcome of either? It was a more fraught weekend even than 24–27 May, when Halifax had defied Churchill and asked Mussolini to intervene. It was the weekend that settled Halifax's fate as Prime Minister.

Halifax assembled an emergency meeting of the War Cabinet at 10 a.m. on the Saturday morning. In front of each member were translated transcripts of Hitler's Reichstag speech and of a much more aggressive document. This had been obtained by MI6, was dated 16 July, addressed from the Führer's Headquarters and labelled Top Secret. Its title was 'Directive No.16 on the Preparation of a Landing Operation against England'. It said:

> Since England, despite her militarily hopeless situation, still shows no willingness to come to terms, I have decided to prepare a landing operation against England, and if necessary to carry it out. The aim of the operation is to eliminate the English home-land as a base for the carrying on of the war against Germany, and, if it should become necessary, to occupy it completely.

Halifax said that Hitler's peace terms could certainly not be taken at face value (although they were not spelt out in the Reichstag speech, the War Cabinet knew roughly what they were) nor should Directive No. 16 be any ground for capitu-lation. Nevertheless, he continued, Britain's defences after Dunkirk were in a parlous state. He was not being defeatist but simply candid when he considered that for Britain to fight on alone, even with her Empire, would be to risk heavy defeat. Would it not be preferable, indeed a national duty, to enter negotiations simply to gain time? As a senior member of Chamberlain's former government he was no longer an appeaser – despite his growing reputation as one in the press – but he continued to believe that time was of the essence; time to re-arm, to bring America into the war, to hope that

Hitler would launch his stupendous attack on Russia regardless. To this end, the Prime Minister concluded, he knew that his old friend Lord Lothian, Ambassador to the United States, was that very weekend using his private channels to ascertain precisely what was available from Berlin. What terms could be on offer, Lord Lothian was asking, to 'a proud and unconquered nation'?

This was Halifax speaking as a man of peace but confident of his skills at round-table persuasion. A traditional British diplomat: worldly but aloof, supercilious, prepared to forgo scruples as far as British national interests were at stake, a believer in the special relationship between the English speaking peoples and a detester of the Soviet Union. Some thought at the time this was because his Christian convictions found Bolshevism abhorrent.

Halifax's proposal was courageous because he knew that after Dunkirk the political mood in Britain was turning rapidly against appeasement or any kind of negotiated peace. A front page in the *Daily Mirror* on 28 May written by the influential guerrilla war expert and socialist Tom Wintringham had caused a stir – 'An aroused people: an angry people: an armed people.' Soon after, writing as CATO, three socialist journalists had rushed out *The Guilty Men*, a savage attack by name on all the appeasers who were now fighting a half-hearted war. Halifax himself was not one of the main targets but he was on the list. It sold nearly 250,000 copies in a matter of days. That very weekend, 21 July, the 'revolutionary patriot' J. B. Priestley encouraged listeners to his BBC *Postscript* talk to occupy vacant houses and gardens owned by those who had fled. Then, also in July, Penguin Books published Tom Wintringham's *New Ways of War*, a practical guide to guerrilla warfare pulled together from his widely read *Picture Post* articles that concluded with a highly provocative last chapter calling for all appeasers to quit the government. It, too, sold like hot cakes. George Orwell summed up the national mood in his book *The English Revolution* written the next year:

> What are the politics of *Picture Post*? Of Priestley's broadcasts, of the *Evening Standard* [Orwell's paper]? They merely point to the existence of multitudes of unlabelled people … for whom war and revolution are inseparable. We cannot establish socialism without defeating Hitler: we cannot defeat Hitler while we remain economically and politically in the nineteenth century.

This sense of revolution was shared by the group of young Conservative politicians who at the end of June had hatched the 'Under-Secretaries Plot'. Harold Macmillan, Robert Boothby and Leo Amery called for the removal of the 'old gang' (Halifax and Chamberlain), a change in the composition of the War Cabinet and the setting up of a Committee of Public Safety. Halifax had persuaded them not to rock the boat but ever since they had goaded Churchill who, of course, was aware how the national mood was changing. After he heard Halifax's proposal for peace negotiations he was incensed; enough was enough.

Churchill repeated the battery of arguments he had fired off that weekend in May: peace and security could not be achieved under a German domination of Europe; that 'even if we were beaten, we should be no worse off than we should be if we were now to abandon the struggle'; that 'the Germans would demand our fleet – that would be called "disarmament" – our naval bases and much else … that we should become a slave state, though a British government which would be Hitler's puppet would be set up'. This time, however, Churchill went further. He said that if the Prime Minister insisted on answering Hitler's speech with an acceptance of negotiation then he would call for Halifax's resignation. Attlee and Greenwood concurred and Chamberlain remained silent. Mindful of the support that Churchill's speech had received in Cabinet on 28 May and that the tide of public opinion was flowing against 'the old gang' with the label of appeasement that it carried, Halifax realised that no amount of rational argument or arm-twisting would work.

The next day, at 9.15 in the evening, Halifax was at the microphone in Broadcasting House, aware that Germany was listening. Just before he went on air he received a phone call from Lord Lothian in the States saying that he had received another approach from Germany. Halifax cut him short. Speaking with his usual bad delivery, for he had suffered from a stutter and hated the 'modern appurtenances of democracy', the Prime Minister said: 'We shall not stop fighting until freedom, for ourselves and others, is secure.' In Britain the speech was well received. In Germany Goebbels called it 'a war crime'.

On Tuesday 23 July, Halifax told the War Cabinet that he intended to resign and would inform the full Cabinet and the King later in the day. The time of the conciliator was over; that of the warrior was about to begin.

Prime Minister Mosley and the United States of Europe

Nigel Jones

The crowded Brighton Dome was as hushed as a Church, or a theatre before the curtain goes up. To increase the dramatic effect, the lights were dimmed and only a powerful single spotlight stabbed down on the empty speaker's podium. Suddenly, a cluster of lights cut through the darkness and focused on the curtains at the back of the hall. The heavy velvet drapes fluttered, as if stirred by a gathering wind, and a tall, dark figure, haloed in white light, strode down the central aisle, staring straight ahead, a slight limp reminding the delegates of his heroic record in the war in which many of them had also served.

Gaining momentum as he approached the platform, the man – 'lithe as a panther' as an admiring journalist wrote later – leapt rather than climbed on to the stage and in a single movement grasped the speaker's lectern with both hands as if he wanted to tear it out of the floor and fling it into the crowd. He radiated determination and aggression. There had been gasps of surprise – and, from the younger women, admiration not unmixed with a more basic emotion – when he had made his abrupt entrance, and thousands of eyes, glistening in excitement, were fixed upon him.

The atmosphere was crackling as though electrically charged. Motionless, the speaker stood up straight, jaw clenched tight, chin thrust forward like a ship's prow, his handsome face with its brilliantined hair and pencil-thin moustache pale in the spotlight. He regarded them silently, almost arrogantly, waiting for the sound of his own voice to split the tense silence. Then the tension snapped. 'Comrades!' he roared, his cut-glass, upper-class accent pronouncing the egalitarian word as 'Cumrades!' Love him or loathe him, Sir Oswald Ernald Mosley Bart had the Labour Party's full attention.

Mosley had never found it difficult to attract attention – that was part of his problem, and a large part of his disturbing appeal. In the short history of the Labour Party, there had never been anyone remotely like him. Born in 1896 as the latest product of a long line of feudal Staffordshire squires, Mosley's natural affiliations of class had been with the Tory Party. Several of his ancestors had been Tory MPs, and his public school upbringing at Winchester, followed by officer training at Sandhurst military academy, had seemed to confirm his conventional career path as a member of the Conservative ruling caste. The two factors that changed this apparently inevitable progression, however, were Mosley's own unruly personality, and – in August 1914 – the outbreak of the First World War.

As the son of a weak, drunken, absentee father and a doting, frustrated mother, Mosley – always called 'Tom' by his family and friends to distinguish him from his father, another Oswald – had slipped early and easily into the role of alpha male. His mother, Lady Katherine Mosley, called him her 'man-child' and spoiled him rotten. Although no friend of the Jews, as a well-read man Mosley must have been aware of Sigmund Freud's dictum that any man who has enjoyed from infancy the unfettered love of his mother will stride down the road of life as a king. Certainly his own life would bear out the truth of the great psychologist's observation. Mosley's unwavering confidence in his own abilities to overcome or sweep aside any problem was at once his making – and his downfall.

Money had never been a problem for the Mosleys – much of their wealth deriving from the ground rents on land that would, with the explosion of the nineteenth-century Industrial Revolution, become greater Manchester. This cushion of cash further bolstered Mosley's self-esteem, causing him to feel that he was above the rules and regulations that governed and restrained lesser mortal men. Mosley's character was riven with contradictions. A sportsman whose interests ranged from rat-fighting and watching naked women wrestle in mud to more conventional fencing and polo; he was no mean intellectual, reading voraciously all from ancient philosophy and history to modern theories of economics and government. Furiously energetic in the pursuit of his political aims, he was at the same time, as contemporary wit Lord Birkenhead perceptively remarked, 'a perfumed popinjay in scented boudoirs' – a frivolous playboy enjoying a leisured lifestyle, an incorrigible womaniser and chaser after other men's wives who was addicted to adultery.

When war broke out in 1914, Mosley was experiencing one of the many awkward career twists that punctuated his life. He had just been suspended from Sandhurst for organising a raid on another officer cadet's room in a row over a polo pony, which had ended with Mosley falling from a window and breaking an ankle. Within weeks, however, Britain was at war and he was recalled to the ranks. Trained, even half-trained, officers with the 'right' background were in short supply, and Mosley joined the elite 16th Lancers and was posted to Dublin to complete his training. Desperate to see action before the fighting ended, Mosley applied for a transfer to the infant Royal Flying Corps. In the typically contradictory and impatient fashion that would characterise his whole career he was leaping horses in midstream, jumping from the cavalry, belonging firmly in the military past, to a branch of the armed forces which to him embodied a mechanised future of speed, modernity and ruthless efficiency: aviation.

Despite his professed admiration for all things contemporary and up to date, Mosley was a hopeless aviator. A technophobe who believed in leaving the nuts and bolts of aircraft engineering to the 'rude mechanicals' on the ground, his early experience as an observer flying behind a pilot was hampered by his inability to distinguish salient objects from the air. When he finally obtained his pilot's license, he crash landed while attempting a 'stunt' before his adoring mother, and once again broke a leg. Rapidly returning to his old regiment in the trenches before the injury was properly healed, Mosley's leg swelled and rotted in the rain and mud until he passed out with the pain. Packed back to Blighty, his front-line service had lasted less than six months, but the glamour of being a former fighting man – however briefly – on both land and air continued to cling to him. His uniform, Byronic limp and handsome looks earned him the admiration of the ladies in and out of the bedroom. Moreover he could, with some credibility, claim to be a spokesman for the war generation – impatient, like his comrades, to create a new and better world in the future, throwing over the old order which had caused the war.

Mosley's home duties at the War Office in Whitehall were not onerous, and allowed him plenty of time to pursue both an active social and sexual life, and his developing political ambition. Courted by both the Tory and Liberal parties to become a parliamentary candidate, he chose the Conservative option not from any particular ideological motive, but because the two safe Tory seats offered were in his native Staffordshire and Harrow, conveniently placed for partying in London. In the end the Harrow seat came up first and Mosley stood there in the 'Coupon Election' that followed the end of the war in December 1918. Although Mosley was officially a supporter of Lloyd George's Tory-dominated coalition, the manifesto on which Mosley was elected was very much a personal agenda. Indeed, much of it sounded like the Fabian socialism that he would soon adopt. Symbolically – and significantly – even the campaign rosettes he sported were deepest red rather than Tory true blue. His policy proposals mixed radical calls for the nationalisation of key economic sectors (land, transport and electricity), slum clearance and state help for educating students and ex-servicemen with a nationalist programme of tariff protection for British goods, outlawing 'alien' foreign immigration and promoting the unity of the British Empire. This platform – which it would not be unfair to call National Socialism – would remain Mosley's bedrock political posture until his dying day.

Triumphantly returned on polling day with a majority of 11,000 over an elderly independent Tory opponent, the 22-year-old Mosley took his seat in the post-war Commons as the House's 'baby', its youngest member. But despite his youth, he soon made his presence felt. Characteristically impatient for 'action' to tackle the post-war malaise, which was already showing signs of high unemployment and a stagnant economy, Mosley shocked his Tory party elders by calling for a new consensus politics. Rejecting party labels as outmoded, Mosley demanded managerial, technocratic solutions to new problems in a world transformed by the war.

Increasingly disillusioned by most of his ageing parliamentary colleagues – described by future Tory Prime Minister Stanley Baldwin as 'hard-faced men who look as if they have

done well out of the war' – and by the slow-moving workings
of parliamentary democracy, Mosley adopted fervently idealistic and progressive positions on many of the great issues of the
day, particularly on foreign affairs and the dirty war in Ireland.

He was an impassioned supporter of the League of Nations,
seeing collective security as the best guarantee against a renewal
of the war that had decimated his own generation. He casti-
gated the military intervention of the Western allies in Russia's
Civil War. He denounced the Amritsar massacre of hundreds
of unarmed Indians ordered by British General Reginald
Dyer. Above all, he spearheaded a spirited Commons campaign against the government's bloody attempt to prevent an
independent Ireland by armed force. After a majority of Sinn
Fein MPs had been elected in December 1918, on a platform
of rejecting the Westminster Parliament and British rule and
forming their own national assembly in Dublin, a guerrilla war
broke out all over southern Ireland. Attacks by the IRA on
Crown Forces were answered by increasingly indiscriminate
reprisals, carried out by rough, tough British ex-servicemen
known as the Black and Tans.

Mosley expressed his sympathy for the Irish struggle for
self-determination and his disgust at the government's response
in passionate and extravagant oratory which excited furious
debate in the House. He assailed the government he had been
elected to support, accusing it of 'a promiscuous devastation of
whole communities reminiscent of the pogroms of the more
barbarous Slavs'. He told ministers that they would not restore
order in Ireland 'by pulling old women out of their beds and
burning their houses'. Mosley's eloquent interventions were
greeted with an embarrassed silence on his side of the House,
but with delighted cheers from the opposition Liberal and
Labour benches.

On 3 November 1920, just two years after being elected as a Tory, Mosley's Irish interventions reached a dramatic climax when he crossed the floor of the House and took his seat as an Independent on the opposition Liberal and Labour benches. Freed from the pretence of supporting an administration he had never had much time for, his attacks on Lloyd George's front bench became ever more savage. Mosley aligned himself with leading intellectuals of the left when he became secretary of a pressure group, the Peace with Ireland Council, whose supporters included the socialists G. D. H. Cole and Ramsay MacDonald. The Council's reports and Mosley's continued parliamentary agitation helped create the climate of opinion that forced Lloyd George to open talks with the Sinn Fein leadership, leading to the 1921 Treaty creating the Irish Free State.

Mosley's Irish campaign had caused him some social embarrassment amidst the overwhelmingly Tory high society set in which he moved. In 1920 he had married Lady Cynthia 'Cimmie' Curzon, a rich heiress and youngest daughter of the high Tory Foreign Secretary, George Nathaniel Curzon. Their wedding in the Chapel Royal had been the social event of the London season, with King George V and Queen Mary topping the guest list. Mosley's defection, however, led to a breach with his father-in-law which was never healed. Mosley was rich enough and confident enough to ignore such ructions. And, in place of those from his own class who would never forgive his 'desertion' as he began his leftwards trajectory, there were a whole new band of friends and admirers who welcomed the glamorous new recruit.

Take, for example Beatrice Webb, the Queen Bee of the Fabian Society and the exemplar of high-minded left-wing thought. After meeting Mosley in the early 1920s she gushed in her journal:

We have made the acquaintance of the most brilliant man in the House of Commons. 'Here is the perfect politician who is also the perfect gentleman' said I to myself as he entered the room … this young person would make his own way in the world [even] without his adventitious advantages, which are many – birth, wealth and a beautiful aristocratic wife. He is also an accomplished orator in the old grand style, and an assiduous worker in the modern manner – keeps two secretaries supplying him with information, but realises that he himself has to do the thinking!

In October 1922, Tory MPs revolted against their leaders who remained under the spell of the Welsh wizard, Lloyd George, and brought down the coalition. In the ensuing election Mosley stood again in Harrow under his Independent label, and fought off a ferocious campaign by his former Tory party comrades to unseat him. (Mosley was forced to sue his Tory opponent for libel after the candidate accused him of inciting Irishmen and Indians to revolt against British rule.) Despite the abuse, Mosley was again returned with a reduced but still substantial majority of 7,422. Nationally, the Tories remained the biggest party with 345 seats, while the Liberals continued their slow but steady decline. The election's real winners were Labour who saw their MPs leap up from sixty-three to 142. Mosley, representing only himself as a party of one, began to believe that here was the wave of the future which he could either ride or drown in.

Mosley's mind was finally made up for him at the next election a year later in November 1923, coming after a change in the Tory leadership, in which a mortally sick Bonar Law resigned to be succeeded by Stanley Baldwin, a pragmatic businessman who was preferred over Mosley's estranged father-in-law, Curzon. This time the Tories lost 100 seats and their overall majority, while Labour continued their rise, for the first time overtaking the Liberals to become the second largest party with 191 seats. The veteran Liberal leader, H. H. Asquith, decided that Labour had earned their chance to govern and backed a minority Labour administration under Ramsay MacDonald – the first in British history. Mosley, a friend of both Asquith and MacDonald, was again returned in Harrow, with his majority cut to just 4,646. He could see which way the tide was running. On 27 March 1924, after making a slashing attack on the Tories as a 'panic-stricken plutocracy' whose policy was 'drift buoyed up by drivel', Mosley applied to join Labour. 'The army of progress', he portentously proclaimed, '… has struck its tents and is on the march.'

If in leaving the Conservatives Mosley had shocked his more staid friends and relations, by actually joining Labour he appalled and shook them to their Tory core. The difference between the wealthy few and the many poor was seen not only in obscure tables of statistics, but in the clothes, food and houses of the two nations. Born into the plusher regions of the upper crust by, as he put it in his application for party membership to MacDonald, 'ranging myself beneath your standard' Mosley had done more than change his party label; he had betrayed his own caste and joined the class enemy.

His new comrades were bedazzled and bemused by their posh new recruit. No one in Labour had ever met anyone like Mosley, still less been expected to welcome them into 'this great movement of ours'. Although the party boasted the odd recruit from the upper crust – the pottery magnate Josiah Wedgwood, for example – Labour's leadership was firmly in the hands of the working class, and was all too conscious of it. As J. R. Clynes, one of their founders, mused with cringe-making servility as the first Labour Cabinet attended George

V to kiss hands at Buckingham Palace: 'As we stood waiting for His Majesty amidst the gold and crimson of the palace, I could not help marvelling at the strange turn of fortune's wheel which had brought [Ramsay] MacDonald the starveling clerk, [J. H.] Thomas the engine driver, [Arthur] Henderson the foundry labourer and [J. R.] Clynes the mill hand to this pinnacle with this man whose forebears had been kings for generations.' What could Mosley possibly have in common with these people?

Many in Mosley's elevated social circle asked themselves the same question. But Mosley had no doubts. He hailed the illegitimate 'starveling clerk' MacDonald as 'the leader of the forces of progress in their assault upon the powers of reaction'. Beneath the flattering rhetoric, however, Mosley was coldly calculating. Never one to underestimate his own abilities, he looked around at the dim, elderly, shabby suited, respectable Labour leaders and favourably compared himself to them. Young, rich, glamorous, courageous, sharp. Why, all he would have to do would be wait for five years, ten at most, and the leadership would fall into his hands like a ripe plum.

Mosley set about seducing – not literally, for his impressive array of mistresses always came from the upper classes – his new party. His particular target was the new Prime Minister, Ramsay MacDonald, whose youthful firebrand socialism had degenerated into pathetic snobbery and slavering worship of the rich and titled. Mosley began to invite MacDonald on week-ends at his new country house, Savehay Farm near Denham in Buckinghamshire, and even accompanied him on fact-finding tours of European capitals to brief the under-educated Scot in the rudiments of great power politics. But Mosley's seductiveness went wider than his party leader and involved his wife

Cimmie who became his partner in a Clintonesque power couple blitz.

Although their millionaire recruits enchanted many of the party faithful, the sniping from envious but less well-heeled potential Labour rivals of Mosley's generation like Hugh Dalton and Herbert Morrison was vicious, and the broadsides from the Tories he had left behind were no less embittered. The *Daily Mail*, vitriolic in its denunciations of champagne socialists, savaged Mosley in his matinee idol mode at another public meeting. 'Mosley, caressing his miniature moustache with one hand and gaily slapping his razor-like trouser leg with the other, beamed delightedly at the girls.' With its familiar *faux* naivety the *Mail* demanded to know when 'Comrade' Mosley was going to drop his title, and when Lady Cynthia would donate her ropes of pearls and diamonds to the deserving poor.

Incurring the wrath of the *Mail* has never hurt an aspiring Labour politician. Mosley's popularity with the party faithful soared. So much so that, abandoning the comfort zone of his Harrow seat, he challenged the future Tory Prime Minister, Neville Chamberlain, in his Birmingham Ladywood bastion in the general election of autumn 1924 after the Liberals pulled the rug from under MacDonald's short-lived first administration. After a hard-found campaign Mosley lost, although he cut Chamberlain's majority to just seventy-seven. Out of Parliament, he decided to re-charge his intellectual batteries by touring the world to find out how other countries were dealing with the growing scourge of unemployment. He visited India and the US, where he stayed with the rising hope of progressive Democrats, F. D. Roosevelt, like Mosley a moneyed patrician who had abandoned his Republican class and embraced the politics of the poor.

Mosley returned a convinced Keynesian. Only by resolute

state action in pumping money into sick and stalled economies could people be employed on vast New Deal-style programmes of public works, and the wheels of industry start to spin again, he announced. Together with a young Marxist disciple, John Strachey, he wrote a tract, *Revolution by Reason*, embodying his new thinking. Meanwhile Mosley was leading a double life: entertaining his louche friends at his country home at weekends; pounding Labour platforms and winning support for his Keynesian views during the week. He skilfully combined the roles of playboy and people's tribune, although he acquired a powerful new Labour enemy in the shape of Philip Snowden, its orthodox economic expert, to whom Mosley's Keynesian views were as much an affront as his wealthy, leisured background.

Mosley was most liked by working-class Labour; most resented by its middle-class members. Socialists like Scotland's Jimmy Maxton or Wales's Nye Bevan admired him, while Morrison and Snowden continued to criticise him as a johnny-come-lately scion of the idle rich who had never done a day's real toil in his life. By the end of the 1920s Mosley had built his own local power base in Birmingham, using Mosley money to finance his return to the Commons in a by-election in Smethwick. And when Baldwin called an election in May 1929 Mosley was returned with an increased majority, along with John Strachey at nearby Aston and another supporter, Allan Young, in Ladywood. Loyal Cimmie, standing in Stoke, was also swept to Westminster on the incoming Labour tide.

For the second time, MacDonald was summoned to the palace to form a Labour government, this time with a small but comfortable majority. Mosley hoped that his cultivation of his leader would be rewarded with a top Cabinet job – perhaps even Foreign Secretary. He was to be disappointed: he got the post of Chancellor of the Duchy of Lancaster, a non-Cabinet, non-portfolio job with a special brief to think the unthinkable about unemployment and find ways of eliminating it. Mosley set to work with a will. By the end of the summer recess he had come up with a bold plan to increase old age pensions in order to encourage early retirement and let young people into employment – but the Cabinet rejected the idea. His next scheme was a Keynesian plan for public works to raise a loan to finance a massive road building programme. Once again the scheme was stymied – this time by his ministerial superior, J. H. Thomas, who as a railway man had no wish to encourage rival roads. Mosley's implacable party enemies (Snowden at the Treasury and Morrison at the Transport Ministry) also weighed in to kill the idea.

Mosley rapidly realised that, far from the dynamic engine of change that he envisaged, the MacDonald government was tired, timid and bankrupt of ideas before it had started. Nothing imaginative or radical could be expected from these extinct volcanoes. So, just as he had built his own power base in Birmingham, he set about broadening his support in the party at large, portraying himself as the dynamic force for the future who would actually do something about unemployment – in stark contrast, he implied, to the dead wood in the Cabinet who merely danced to Capital's tune. His aggressive attack on capitalism – at a time when the effects of the great Wall Street crash of October 1929 were just beginning to be felt in the lengthening dole queues – won Mosley thousands of new Labour friends, particularly in the unions and the swelling ranks of the jobless. By March 1930, unemployment had rocketed to 1,700,000, and Mosley stood head and shoulders above his Labour colleagues as the only politician who appeared ready to conquer it.

This was reflected in the 'Mosley Memorandum', a

fifteen-page document that he circulated to the Prime Minister and his Cabinet in January. Approved by J. M. Keynes himself, the paper amounted to the most radical economic proposals ever laid before a British government. The Memorandum repeated Mosley's rejected proposals for early retirement pensions and publicly-financed road building; recommended the creation of a government industrial bank to channel funds into work creation schemes; and proposed a small Cabinet to direct the battle against the slump on the lines of Lloyd George's five-man War Cabinet.

Couched in moderate language, Mosley's proposals were similar to the New Deal that his friend FDR was about to launch in America after his victory in the 1932 presidential elections. But the MacDonald government would have none of it. Snowden predictably denounced it as 'Bolshevism gone mad' and after being shuffled around the Cabinet it was kicked into the long grass for a Cabinet sub-committee to consider (and doubtless reject) at leisure.

Briefly, Mosley considered resignation. He even, it was rumoured, had it in mind to quit Labour altogether and form his own 'New Party' to campaign for a fresh activist politics. If such reports were true, they never got beyond saloon bar – or salon – gossip. Mosley listened instead to the wiser counsels of friends like the moderate Tory, Bob Boothby, who told him that new parties had no hope in Britain. He need only curb his impatience for a short time until the party leadership fell into his lap and he found himself leading 'a moderate government of the left'. And so it came to pass.

Mosley's capture of the Labour Party leadership was a reflection of the depths of the crisis afflicting Britain – and the world – during the great Depression of the 1930s. Only from a sense of desperation did the moderate and even conservative masses comprising the party faithful turn to a man like Mosley, a wealthy aristocrat offering radical and untried solutions to their distress. Frustrated by his inability to persuade the party's leadership to adopt his proposals, Mosley turned to backbench MPs, building up a 'Mosley mob' of some 100 members, led by Nye Bevan, who pressed the leadership to adopt his platform. His campaign was underpinned by, among others, Labour's intellectual house journal, the *New Statesman*.

Support for Mosley extended well beyond Labour's ranks. Left-wing Tory MPs such as the future Prime Minister Harold Macmillan, another war veteran whose conscience had been stricken by the plight of the jobless in his Stockton constituency, hovered on the verge of endorsing Mosley. Other Tories such as Oliver Stanley, Henry Mond and Walter Elliott expressed approval too. Among the liberals and future ministers, Archibald Sinclair and Leslie Hore-Belisha lent their support. Buoyed by the knowledge that he had the younger, braver and more intelligent elements of his party and country firmly on his side, Mosley went to the October 1930 Labour conference in Llandudno determined to stake his claim to the future.

In a hard-hitting quarter-hour speech, all the more effective for its brevity, Mosley outlined his plans to the conference. Labour, he roared, must force banks to invest in reconstruction rather than sending their money abroad or squirreling it away to gather dust in their vaults. Britain's fragile home markets must be shielded from the firestorm of the Depression by building tariff walls against cheap foreign imports. An action programme should stimulate work and demand and get cash moving again. Above all, Mosley concluded, it was Labour's task not to shirk the challenge of beating the Depression. The left-wing MP Fenner Brockway, hitherto no Mosley fan, described his speech as receiving the greatest ovation he had ever heard at a party conference, while the ultra-Tory *Morning Post* newspaper hailed Mosley as the 'Moses' who would lead Labour out of the wilderness. Delegates clapped, they stamped, they cheered. Although Mosley's motion urging adoption of his measures was defeated by the undemocratic block votes of the unions, Mosley had put down his marker for the future, and the party knew where to look for its leader if push came to shove.

Meanwhile, Mosley continued to build his Labour constituency. Two days after Llandudno, he addressed a Merseyside rally, with the massive bulk of Ernie Bevin, boss of the powerful Transport Workers, sitting reassuringly beside him. He was cheered to the echo when he called for the party to show 'an iron will' to cope with the coming crisis. With Bevin backing him among the union bosses and Nye Bevan organising the 'Mosley mob' in the parliamentary party, Mosley felt renewed confidence that he was on the right path.

The crisis that Mosley had long anticipated exploded with sudden ferocity in August 1931. The collapse of the Austrian Kredit Anstalt bank triggered a massive haemorrhage of confidence in the banking system. That seeping away of trust became a deluge when the MacDonald government learned that US financiers would not bail out Britain's embattled economy unless huge cuts were implemented, including a drastic 20 per cent slashing of the already meagre dole paid to the unemployed. Aghast, and running from his responsibilities, MacDonald scuttled to the Palace to resign. But the King had already secured the agreement of the Tories and Liberals to join a 'national' government under MacDonald's nominal leadership. His vanity tickled, MacDonald, along with Snowden and J. H. Thomas, agreed to the coalition.

The rest of the Labour Party rose in revolt against MacDonald's 'treacherous sell-out'. Backbench MPs and Labour's rank and file branded the Prime Minister and the tiny rump who backed him as traitors betraying the ordinary people who had raised them to ermined eminence. Ironically, as the 'national' government prepared to go to the country to ask for a mandate to rule, its platform included the very proposals for public spending to finance recovery that Mosley had been vainly advocating. The prophet was at last recognised by those who had spurned him.

But the October 1931 election that followed was a triumph for the new national government – and a disaster for Labour, who were almost wiped out by the coalition tide and reduced to just fifty-five seats. The party leadership was decimated: MacDonald, Snowden and Thomas were now 'Tory stooges' – in office, but not in power – and of those Labourites who had survived the rout, only three stood out: George Lansbury, a venerable and honourable old pacifist warhorse, who was elected leader by default, and the mousy East End MP Clement Attlee, who became his deputy. But the clear coming man – returned in his Birmingham bastion – was none other than Sir Oswald Mosley.

The early 1930s were harsh years. At home, despite the government's belated attempts to revive the economy, unemployment remained at shamefully high levels, devastating a generation. Abroad, Hitler's Nazis came to power in Germany and Mussolini's Italian Fascists launched a brutal attack on Abyssinia, Africa's last independent state. There was little that Labour could do to stop the rot, especially after one of its founding components, the left-wing Independent Labour Party, disaffiliated. This was Mosley's chance: a weakened party was his for the taking. By 1935 he had built a formidable twin power base in what was left of the Parliamentary Party and in the unions. Nye Bevan and Ernie Bevin had swallowed their doubts about Mosley's lack of socialist and working-class credentials and, recognising his enormous public appeal, had thrown their considerable weight behind him.

Mosley transformed and modernised Labour's style. Gone were down-at-heel party gatherings of shabby men in dingy pubs. In came mass rallies in enormous public stadiums like Olympia and Earl's Court. Carefully choreographed, these events featured marching bands, drum corps, spotlights and dramatic music, all leading to a climax when the speaker, usually Mosley himself, addressed a crowd which had been worked up to fever pitch. Many old Labourites murmured that Mosley had taken a leaf out of Hitler and Goebbels' books, but Mosley replied that the people liked drama and theatre. Their own drab lives distinctly lacked these qualities and the rallies brought in the punters. He was right: party membership soared and Mosley's star shone anew. His electrifying oratory, when he inveighed against the 'do nothing' National govern-ment, and the 'old gangs' who kept their arthritic hands on the levers of power, convinced many that he was the man of destiny who would lead Labour out of its wilderness. Apart from his Birmingham bastion, he was especially popular in the East End of London, where he drummed home a message of 'British jobs for British workers'.

Mosley's patriotic protectionism had resonance with workers – such as the cotton industry in Lancashire and the wool mills in Yorkshire – who saw their once mighty products shrivelling in the face of foreign competition. His rural background made him a convincing advocate of the countryside in the grip of a massive agricultural slump. His war record and calls for 'action' and 'discipline' impressed the millions of ex-servicemen who had served like him in the war; his suave looks, glamour and style dazzled impressionable younger women unimpressed by the distinctly seedy appearance of his party rivals: balding bespectacled Attlee and one-eyed Morrison. Above all, his thundering oratory and evident determination clawed at the emotions of voters bored and disillusioned by grey, tired old men like Baldwin and MacDonald. Mosley had brought excitement – and perhaps an edge of danger – back into politics, making it (like the movies) a new branch of popular entertainment. And, as the cherry on the cake, Mosley garnered a huge sympathy vote in May 1933 when his long-suffering wife Cimmie, almost as popular in the party as her unfaithful husband, died of peritonitis. Now Mosley, the eligible widower bringing up three children apparently alone, had another attraction.

The climax of Mosley's campaign to bring Labour back into play – and win power for himself – came at the 1935 party conference in Brighton's Dome when a devastating attack by Mosley's ally Ernie Bevin on the party's sheepish old leader, George Lansbury, climaxed with Bevin's wounding accusation that the old man, who with his mutton-chop whiskers resembled a throwback to the nineteenth century, was 'hawking his pacifist conscience round the party waiting for someone to buy it'. Cut to the quick, Lansbury resigned, and was replaced as interim leader by his deputy, Clement Attlee. But the mousy, pipe-smoking Major Attlee, a decent man with an impressive war record, was no match for Mosley in seizing the public's imagination.

Where Mosley was loud, Attlee was quiet; while Mosley had glamour, Attlee was dull; Mosley lapped up the limelight as though he were a film star; Attlee shunned it, giving the impression that he was in politics by accident and didn't much enjoy it. In the general election of 1935 Labour's fortunes were partially restored – they won back 100 of the seats they had lost in 1931, but even so the hated national government won a resounding majority. Had he been leader, Mosley indicated, Labour would have performed much more impressively.

The disappointing election gave Mosley his chance. Impatient for power and unimpressed by the modest Major Attlee, the party held a leadership election. Although Attlee led in the early rounds, the other candidates Arthur Greenwood and Herbert Morrison were progressively eliminated, and their votes went overwhelmingly to Mosley. In the final round, he pipped Attlee by just three votes. In the few years of uneasy peace that remained, Mosley concentrated on the increasingly alarming state of foreign affairs. Controversially he visited Mussolini in Rome and Hitler in Berlin. He praised the two dictators for eliminating unemployment with the public works he favoured, but was careful to insist that such dictatorial methods were 'alien' to the British way of life. Meanwhile, he urged the necessity for re-armament on a reluctant and tight-fisted national government. Mosley gave Labour a new slogan: 'Minding Britain's Business'. By expanding the Territorial Army, investing in new projects like the Spitfire fighter and new defence technology such as radar, he insisted Britain would at the same time make itself invulnerable to foreign invasion and give work to its army of unemployed. In full action man mode, Mosley was photographed and filmed climbing into and flying a Spitfire, firing a machine-gun on a TA army range, descending a coal mine and rolling out blazing sheet metal in a steel mill.

When war came in 1939 Mosley was at the forefront of those urging a more vigorous prosecution of hostilities. He attacked his old opponent Neville Chamberlain in typical style as 'an unctuous, umbrella-wielding undertaker who wants to bury Britain' and threw Labour's support unhesitatingly behind Winston Churchill when he formed a new coalition in May 1940. Given responsibility for the Home Front as Churchill's deputy, Mosley spearheaded formation of the Home Guard, and oversaw the building of coastal defences in the dangerous summer of 1940 when invasion was hourly awaited. Film footage still exists of Mosley touring the barbed beaches, Mosley throwing a hand grenade in a Home Guard training exercise, and Mosley inspecting bomb damage in his beloved East End at the height of the Blitz. As a broadcaster he rivalled Churchill in his roars of defiance, summoning up Britain's glorious past as he vowed vengeance on 'the Nazi beasts who have dared to raise their hands against us'. Keeping the two outsize egos of Churchill and Mosley from fatally falling out was a job that fell to Mosley's loyal deputy, Clem Attlee.

Away from the cameras and microphones, Mosley established a 'Brains Trust' of his supporters to draw up a blueprint for a post-war Labour Britain. The philosopher C. E. M. Joad and the novelist J. B. Priestley were placed in charge of broadcasting; Michael Foot chaired the committee on culture and the Press; while the young don Richard Crossman wrote Labour's manifesto 'Let Us Face The Future'. J. M. Keynes, no less, framed the economic programme which called for the public ownership of vital industries. Always impatient with party labels, Mosley used his pre-war contacts such as the progressive Tory Harold Macmillan to devise a modern foreign policy that called for the unification of Europe to prevent more fratricidal wars.

When victory over Germany was finally achieved in May 1945, Mosley wasted no time in demanding an election. He portrayed the campaign as a generational struggle between

Churchill who, he pointed out, was an old-fashioned Victorian imperialist, steeped in the outmoded thinking of the nineteenth century; and himself, twenty years younger, a modern man determined to drag Britain into the late twentieth century and build 'a cleaner, juster, prouder, greater Britain – a land, at last, owned by its people and forging its own future' as he put it in the great speech that climaxed the campaign. The results, when they came in, shocked those who had expected an easy victory for the wartime Prime Minister. It was a Labour landslide. Still only fifty, Sir Oswald Mosley had finally achieved the position he had assumed was his rightful destiny since his childhood. He was Prime Minister.

When political historians of the early twenty-first century looked back at the dynamic decade of the 1945–55 Labour government led by Sir Oswald Mosley, it acquired in hindsight an air of inevitability. Its three major achievements – reconstruction of British industry, European federation and de-colonisation – were the tripod upon which the stability, prosperity and the confidence that characterised British society for the rest of the century were founded upon. Until his death in 1980, Mosley was fondly remembered as the founding father of a new Britain, much like de Gaulle in France, and, alongside his wartime partner, Churchill, as the greatest Prime Minister of the twentieth century.

The Britain that Mosley inherited in 1945 was exhausted by war and near-bankrupt. Mosley saw that the days of Europe as the mighty continent dominating the rest of the world were over. The only way that his country and the continent as a greater whole could continue to exert an influence and pull its weight in the world was to pool its resources, put aside the destructive quarrels of the past that had devastated the globe in two world wars, and devote its brains and energy to constructing a new nation: Europe. The result of Mosley's advocacy was the 1948 Treaty of London, in which the leading powers of western Europe (France, West Germany, Italy and the Benelux countries) joined in establishing a new confederation, scrapping outmoded tariff barriers and borders, allowing free movement of labour within Europe, and building the nucleus of a united European armed force. Today's United States of Europe is the result of Mosley's vision.

Mosley saw the destruction wrought by the war as a challenge and an opportunity for rebuilding rather than a daunting problem. One of his first acts as Premier was to send his friend J. M. Keynes to Washington to negotiate a new post-war financial and economic order that would, as he promised, eliminate 'the insane cycle of boom and bust that characterised capitalism'. He derided the free market system as 'the economics of the monkey house' which had suited the go-getting society of nineteenth-century entrepreneurs, but had no place in a complex, sophisticated, technologically driven late twentieth-century world. Mosley saw to it that Britain got its share of the Marshall Plan's largesse and wrung extra funds from Washington by offering the US long leases of 'redundant' British bases around the world, from Gibraltar to the Falklands. He used the money to re-equip British industry and fund such initiatives as the European space programme, which won the race to put a man in space by 1960, and Britain's all-conquering aviation and automobile industries. British Aerospace's takeover of Boeing in 1953 to create the world's biggest plane-building company was the finest fruit of his investment in industry.

Although born into the Victorian era at the acme of imperialism, Mosley essentially had a modern mind and recognised that the era of the 'white man's burden' was over and done. He lost no time in divesting Britain of her Empire, a process that, contrary to the pessimistic predictions of many, was accomplished without significant bloodshed. Indian independence was followed by the freeing of Britain's remaining Asian, African and Caribbean colonies. Mosley's Commonwealth Partnership Programme not only established favourable trade treaties with Britain's former colonies but set a model for the US Peace Corps in sending young Britons out to help in the construction of developing nations. Mosley retained the concept of national service but, to the relief of the Army, drafted young men and women into the partnership programme instead of the armed forces.

The principle of partnership also informed Mosley's domestic agenda. Instead of outright socialist nationalisation, which he now condemned as 'anachronistic', Mosley introduced what he called 'co-ownership' into law. This made it compulsory for companies to put employees on their boards, an idea which both built loyalty to the firm into the workforce's ethic, and curbed what the Prime Minister called 'the wild predations of capital's robber barons'. He energetically cleared the slums that had survived Hitler's bombs and built a chain of new towns, known as 'Mosleyvilles' around London, Birmingham and Manchester. All this was accomplished with the feverish energy and barrage of noisy propaganda that had always been the hallmarks of Mosley's style. In the years that followed his premiership no one fundamentally challenged the consensus that Mosley had established: the generation of baby boomers born in the 1950s were Mosley's children, and the country they lived in was Mosley's Britain.

In the end, it was not his politics but his personality that brought Mosley down. The constant plots by those he called 'my pygmies' – old Labour stalwarts such as Herbert Morrison and Hugh Dalton – to replace him with what they called 'real Labour' began to wear his patience thin. His marriage to the eccentric, right-wing Diana Mitford, the extravagant salons she held with her wealthy friends in Downing Street and above all the publication of outspoken memoirs by his eldest son Nicholas, in which Mosley appeared in a distinctly bad and unflattering light as an arrogant, womanising, racist braggart and bully, combined to undermine his once stratospheric popularity.

After Mosley won the 1950 election with a majority not far short of his 1945 landslide, the ageing Churchill grumpily surrendered the Tory leadership to Anthony Eden, a handsome moustachioed glamour boy war hero in the Mosley mould, and the Tories won a series of by-elections.

After seven years at the top, Mosley's 'New Labour' began to seem tired and old hat. People grew bored of Mosley and finally, and perhaps more importantly, Mosley grew bored with them. His sudden and unexpected resignation in 1955 over a trivial issue – the defeat of his proposal to replace Britain's First Past the Post electoral system with an Alternative Vote – was widely seen as a fit of political pique. For those who knew him well, as he took off to an exile's hedonistic existence in Paris, it was, however, characteristic and typically vintage Mosley: impetuous, dramatic and foolhardy perhaps, but brave.

Prime Minister Morrison and municipal socialism

Eric Midwinter

Incredulous excitement was the dominant mood in Labour committee rooms on 26 July, as the 1945 general election results were announced, with the Labour Party on line for a huge victory. Labour won 393 seats with 47.8 per cent of the votes cast, against 213 Conservative seats (39.8 per cent of the vote) and only 12 Liberal seats (just 9 per cent of the total votes). Labour had a huge working majority of 146.

Yet, in London, at the Labour Party headquarters another more covert drama was played out. The ambitious Herbert Morrison, supported by his close friend Sir Stafford Cripps, leading backbencher Maurice Webb and the 1945 conference chairman, Ellen Wilkinson, was arguing that Clement Attlee, leader of the party, should not accept the premiership. Morrison had told Attlee the day before the election of his intention, whatever the result, to compete for the leadership. Constitutionally he based his case, perhaps somewhat flimsily, on decisions taken at the 1933 conference to prevent the leader from agreeing to form a government without consultation with the party, as Ramsay MacDonald had done in 1931.

The next day Morrison, never one to show a hint of self-consciousness or false modesty, raised the issue at the Administrative Committee of the Parliamentary Labour Party, where he was received with a mixture of groans and cheers. Meanwhile the tiny but formidable Ellen Wilkinson, heroine of the Jarrow hunger march of the 1930s, gathered together the newly elected north-eastern MPs in the Newcastle Station Hotel, prior to them taking the overnight train to London, urging them to support Morrison's cause. Key figures like Stafford Cripps and Aneurin Bevan had, indeed, assumed that there would be a leadership contest. The academic Harold Laski, the party's leading intellectual and then chairman of the National Executive Committee, had also campaigned for a change of leader.

Clement Attlee was a careful and politic man. He had earned much respect for his wartime role as deputy Prime Minister, whereby he had practically run the domestic side of British life, but, laconic and low-key, his deliberate, sparse style had not made so great a popular impact. Although urged by his supporter, Ernest Bevin, to 'get down to the palace quick' and although he said forthrightly that Herbert Morrison's thinking was 'cockeyed', he felt there was some justice in the constitutional view expressed. He was anxious, too, about future plotting, and thought it best to have his position confirmed by election. He bowed to the wishes of his detractors.

When the Labour members gathered later that day, there was a heated argument, with some of the new MPs, a few of them still in military uniform as the war in the Far East was not yet over, bewildered by events. They voted rather unconvincingly for a leadership election, which had, of necessity, to be completed hurriedly. The country sorely needed leadership. The canvassing was hasty, crude and even coarse in fashion – and Herbert Morrison was an expert in that kind of tough political in-fighting. He won by a moderate majority. Within an hour he was speeding to Buckingham Palace to receive the seals of prime ministerial office.

Why had Clement Attlee been overthrown with such apparent ease? There were several factors in Morrison's favour. He was widely regarded as the creator of the London Labour Party's greatness, and was already hailed as one of the most efficacious rulers of a major municipality the world, let alone Britain, had known. Crucially, he was – and remains – the only Labour figure who had reached the top ranks of the party solely through local government. Next, his highly successful wartime service, principally as Home Secretary and Minister for Home Security, had given him a well-merited base. With his perky grasp of public relations – 'Up, Housewives, and at 'em' was one of his famous aphorisms – and his formidable stamina for and skill in administrative matters, he had made a national name for himself. With his unruly quiff and horn-rimmed spectacles, he was a gift for the political cartoonist, and he had rarely been out of the public eye. Finally, he was recognised as the supreme electioneer, principally in his native London, but also nationally. Many MPs recognised that, without him, they might not have made it into Parliament, let alone government.

Faced with the sudden and immediate need to make the difficult choice between the hare and the tortoise, they plumped for the former. And, for all his flaws, Herbert Morrison was an unusual mix of social idealist and political realist, unflinching in his strong reforming beliefs and unfailingly pure in his personal financial dealings, yet adeptly shrewd in his mastery of the mechanics of power and rigorously detailed in his organisational capability.

There were dangers. It could have been a dystopian nightmare, at least for those of a nervous left-wardly inclined disposition. Ernest Bevin's paranoid detestation of Herbert Morrison and the volatile if attractive character of Aneurin Bevan might have fractured a government that struggled on through many post-war vicissitudes. Aspects of the welfare state might have been sadly left undone, while Indian independence might have been lost, with dreadful civil war the likely consequence. The Conservatives might have stormed back earlier and with a larger majority and added assurance. The Socialist dawn could have been a false one.

But it was a utopian dream come true.

On becoming Prime Minister, Herbert Morrison struck out boldly in his choice of Cabinet. Among Attlee's private papers his biographers have found the pencilled list of his intended Cabinet, one that he had discussed with his first lieutenant, Ernest Bevin. It is intriguing to compare the real Morrisonian with the intended Attlean Cabinet. Ever loyal and pragmatic, Attlee agreed to be Foreign Secretary, a task he undertook with due diligence and with none of the likely John Bullish approaches of Bevin, his own suggested incumbent. Largely operating on his own responsibility in a post that Morrison, while aware of its political clout, found uninviting, he was able to guarantee the granting of Indian independence, an issue very close to his heart.

The new Prime Minister persuaded a grudging Ernest Bevin to follow up his immensely significant task as wartime director of labour by becoming Lord Privy Seal and economic overlord, with a particular remit for nationalisation of industries, the role Attlee had earmarked for Morrison. The two men did not get on, but Bevin, like many another politician, realised that the opportunities to attain power and turn long-held ideas into fruition come infrequently. Grumbling incessantly about the loathsome 'erbert, Ernie Bevin, the roly-poly embodiment of working-class solidarity, still remained determined to be the man who socialised British industry.

Another sparklingly unexpected selection was Aneurin

Bevan as Lord President of the Council and leader of the House of Commons. Nye Bevan, who had favoured Herbert Morrison for the leadership, was delighted to oblige, As a gifted parliamentarian, he enjoyed crowing, to the continuous good cheer of the packed benches behind him, over a dismayed opposition and debating ingeniously with its still formidable front bench. He also demonstrated an unforeseen talent in the minutiae of controlling a heavy load of parliamentary business and promoting backbench involvement. Critically, to the minds of several commentators, he was kept somewhat out of the public vision and thus proved less of an electoral hazard in 1950 than might have been the case.

Herbert Morrison did not hesitate to reward his mainline supporter, Sir Stafford Cripps, with the Chancellorship. This upper-class ascetic was easily the most technocratic of the Labour front rank, with an astute comprehension of the linkages of the economic and fiscal systems. Forever associated with post-war 'austerity' and the drive to boost manufacturing industry and the export trade, he steered the economy with frugal effectiveness. His tax regime was marked by unyielding fairness, so much so that, by 1950, the gap between rich and poor was narrower than at any time in British history. It was said at the time that it was narrower than in the Soviet Union. Curiously to the modern eye, this abstemious figure, spectrally gaunt and owl-eyed in appearance, enjoyed remarkable popularity.

Attlee had apparently thought Hugh Dalton should be Chancellor. A boomingly optimistic yet wholly unreliable Old Etonian, and the fifth of the big beasts in the Labour jungle, Morrison believed Dalton's knowledge of the City was cancelled out by his comparative ignorance of business and industry. Morrison offered him the final major post of Home

Secretary. Often a poisoned chalice, it was, in this era, more a bowl of cherries. During the second half of the nineteenth century, the crime rate had dropped by massive proportions, estimated by some analysts has as much as a half. This almost abnormally low rate was sustained through the first part of the twentieth century, principally because the community disciplines of family, street, school, church and work held solid. In fact, the crime rate dropped by a further 5–10 per cent during the Morrison years. The Home Secretaryship proved to be a comfortable posting for Hugh Dalton, a man who turned out to be more interested in politics than administration, and never made a major mark in the Labour government.

With this experimental and idiosyncratic bunch of ministers in place, what turned out to be the highly successful Morrison ministry was characterised by three distinct approaches, each of them firmly based on Herbert Morrison's own inclinations.

In the first place, as to foreign affairs, the new Prime Minister opposed the 'world-power fantasists'. Despite his enormous affection for the British people, he believed, not least given her bankrupt, knackered condition as the result of wartime sacrifices, that the nation could no more be a first-class power. He was much troubled by military expenditure. In the 1914–18 war he had been a conscientious objector, albeit a valiant one, for, given he had lost the sight of an eye at birth, he had had no need to declare himself thus. He was ever watchful of unjustified militancy. He asserted his belief most concisely in 1949, when he argued that military costs 'gravely endanger our economic recovery, on which all else, our defence included, depends. Yet the forces provided would still be inadequate … we are, in fact, in danger of paying more than we can afford for defences that are nevertheless inadequate, or even illusory'.

The position in 1946 was that the armed forces and defence

industries employed 2.35 million people with 500,000 young men annually siphoned off for national service. The 'robber economy' of defence, priced at a yearly £1,300 million meant that the cost of peacetime defence was 15 per cent of GNP, whereas it had only been 7 per cent in 1938, when the country had already started re-arming. As Morrison argued, the armed forces were still not fit for purpose – and the nation was short of 650,000 workers.

The service chiefs, purple with rage at such treatment, continued to make their exorbitant demands, but, under Morrison's leadership, the Colonel Blimps were repulsed. Stafford Cripps was keen to support this view; Clement Attlee was personally no hawk – 'I have become sceptical about Britain's ability to fully maintain itself as a major power', he confided to close friends – and Ernest Bevin, who, many historians believe, would have proved a gung-ho flag-waver, was now on the other side of the argument, saddled with the task of making the post-war economy strong. The new National Service Act was summarily scrapped, to the delight of thousands who found the experience frustrating; the regular services, for whom the purposeless job of training transient recruits was equally tedious, were remodelled as brisk, proficient, professional agencies, ready to move quickly to resolve problems in troublesome areas. When it came to the Korean War, Britain was able quietly to fulfil its United Nations function with the provision of a small but highly expert detachment.

Freed from much of the incubus of military service and expenditure, the British economy was able to flourish and shrug off some of the more austere features of post-war social life rather earlier than might have been the case.

In the second place, as to nationalisation, Morrison himself was the key player. The Labour Party was not well prepared with elaborate plans for taking industries into public ownership, and there was little enthusiasm for any worker or 'syndicalist' control. The chief working model was the 'public corporation' formula that Morrison himself had utilised very satisfactorily in the establishment of the London Transport Board in 1933. The 'board' principle, with government appointees acting as trustees for the corporations, was extensively employed as the coal mines (1947), electricity, gas and the railways (all 1948) were brought into public ownership. It all happened without too much fuss. The railways and mines, after a long war without chance of refurbishment, were in a parlous state and no capitalist would have wanted them. Two-thirds of gas and electricity operations were already in local government hands.

Assisted by his impressive stature in the trade union world, Bevin endeavoured to involve the workforce more closely with the administration of the newly nationalised industries. Morrison himself came to believe that this had been a weakness of the nationalisation programme. He told the TUC in 1948 that 'the real problem ... was that of industrial democracy at lower levels'.

During these years, the critique emerged of undue rigidity and blandness in the 'board' mechanism – and the chief internal critic was the leading actor, Herbert Morrison. In a memorandum in 1947, he wrote, 'we have taken no steps to ensure that the Boards have before them a standard of efficiency and costs', while he continually assailed the selection of mediocre placemen on both national and regional boards. He constantly pleaded with officials to recruit men of 'freshness of vision, initiative and readiness for change'. He especially desired the search to be widened from the metropolis to 'lively and able industrialists in the provinces, Scotland and Wales ... they should not be forgotten'.

With the authority of the premiership behind him and as a former local authority wizard, he also engaged the municipal interest more fluently, hopeful of making the new state services less faceless. While never exaggerating the humane nature of councillors and local officials, Morrison did realise that they were more accessible than anonymous centralised figures. His astute dismantlement of the National Fire Service in 1947 makes for a neat test case. There had been a higgledy-piggledy mess of 1,688 fire brigades in 1941 when he efficiently nationalised them in 1941; when they were conveyed back to the local authorities, he ensured there were just 157 effective county fire forces. That partnership of dedicated municipal involvement and rational central oversight, redolent of the best of Victorian practice, is the key to what Morrison achieved as Prime Minister in this field.

As to the welfare state, Herbert Morrison was equally aware of the potential of the municipality. He knew from experience that, whatever their political colour, councillors and officers were attracted by mainstream responsibilities. During the planning of the National Health Service, he successfully argued for a substantial local government input, not least by the retention of municipal hospitals. This avoided the weakness of some national schemes elsewhere of the separateness of the medical and parallel social services.

It was only natural that he should turn to Ellen Wilkinson to be his Minister for Health. Diminutive, pale, blue-eyed, this bonny Manchester-born fighter was his staunchest supporter and a lady with whom it is seriously alleged he had a long affair. Herbert Morrison had grown largely estranged from his first wife, Margaret, following the very difficult birth of their daughter Mary (later to win retrospective fame as Peter Mandelson's mum) and her refusal to renew marital relations.

Ellen Wilkinson, who retained her fieriness in the face of arduous illness, had been Morrison's wartime parliamentary secretary. She had become known as 'the Shelter Queen' because of her energies in that useful direction, not least in her endorsement of the indoor 'Morrison Shelter'.

The task of creating the National Health Service was the making of Ellen Wilkinson, saving her from a political and personal life overshadowed by disappointment, sickness, depression and even suicidal tendencies. She was re-energised and refreshed to do wondrous things, establishing the centrepiece of the welfare state with shining brilliance. She adopted her mentor's watchword of national/local partnership, leaving the local authority hospitals intact and sweeping the voluntary hospitals into municipal hands. With her natural bent for the well-being of families, she emphasised one aspect of the legislation that might easily have been neglected – the provision of local 'Health Centres', offering comprehensive health treatment. All across the nation there arose Ellen Wilkinson Health Centres, emblems of socialised medicine at its best.

The unsung but highly effective Jim Griffiths took up the reins of National Insurance, as, according to that pencilled list, he would have done had Attlee moved into 10 Downing Street. It was he who delivered the seminal 1948 National Insurance Act. His insistence on immediately raising basic benefits from a weekly 10s (50p) to 26s (130p), against the advice of Sir William Beveridge who cautiously suggested a gradual scale, means that he was genuinely responsible for the only spectacular increase in benefits since the Poor Law was introduced in 1601. In the Morrisonian dispensation, he followed Ellen Wilkinson's example and mediated much of the new social provision through the local authorities. 'Municipalisation' was an important aspect of Morrison's premiership.

In another smart move the Prime Minister split the duties of the Health Ministry, recognising that the NHS and the housing crisis was too big a burden for one minister. Morrison, from his London supremo days, regarded housing as a high priority. He created a separate housing post and offered it to his close associate, the suave and urbane Sir Hartley Shawcross, famed as the UK's leading jurist at the Nuremberg war trials, but acquainted with Herbert Morrison as one of his eleven wartime Regional Commissioners, in charge of civil defence, and, in the event of invasion, regional oversight. An assured administrator, he livened up the housing market, doubling the initial and rather pessimistic original target to a score of 2 million new housing units over five years. This was done, in part, by finding a compromise between the well-intentioned insistence on high standards, hence relatively slow provision, that was favoured by some Labour politicians such as Aneurin Bevan, and the 'rabbit hutch' speedier approach, urged by Conservative members, such as Harold Macmillan. Shawcross worked in cahoots with the very capable Lewis Silkin at the Ministry of Town and Country Planning, who, as well as founding a whole circle of successful new towns, settled an acceptable schedule for planning and land usage for a generation.

At education, Chuter Ede, freed from the desultory days at the Home Office to which Clement Attlee had intended confining him, was given his first love, for it was he, the sensible and thoughtful child of Unitarian shop-keeping stock, who had assisted Rab Butler with the 1944 Education Act that gave secondary education to all. A former teacher of sensible opinions, he had not, like many Labourites, viewed that legislation as the last word on the subject. Among those who thought education needed no further reform was Ellen Wilkinson, pencilled in by Attlee to be his education minister, a post which she would have thought a depressing backwater. Having been a National Union of Teachers officer, Chuter Ede's ear was open to progressive thinking about schools.

Ede was now to be responsible for delivering the ambitious 1944 Act and ensuring a secondary school place for every child of school age. But what he built – a system of grammar schools for the few and secondary moderns for the rest – he never saw as the last word, and criticism mounted about the divisive iniquities of eleven-plus selection. The criticism was technical as well as ethical. It was discovered that, as well as being vulnerable to 'systematic coaching', there was a 10 per cent error in the testing procedure (when the 1960 national service cohort was examined in 1960, it was found that one in four had been wrongly allocated at eleven), while the proportion of grammar school places on offer varied wildly from area to area, with girls suffering an additional numerical handicap. Soon the research into the social class differential would emerge, so that, later, the left-wing educational academic Brian Simon was able to claim that the son of a Carmarthenshire solicitor had 180 times the chance of going to university as the daughter of a West Ham docker. In 1966 it was shown that the proportion of university students who were working class was the same as in 1926.

Chuter Ede, taking much of this to heart, was instrumental in encouraging the development of what was sometimes called the multilateral secondary school (Yew Tree School in Wythenshawe, Manchester was an early instance), while Anglesey, for obvious geographic reasons, was already moving to complete comprehensive reorganisation. Chuter Ede welcomed, with Herbert Morrison's backing, the LCC 'London School Plan' of 1947, inclusive of comprehensive school reform.

The 1950 general election was not fought between the forces of rapid progression and obstinate retrogression, but between the Labour Party, keen to build carefully on moderate social gains, and the Tory Party, prepared to accept the new status quo and, in general, 'conserve' it. Although analysts were ready to scoff that the Labour government had missed the opportunity to radicalise society and that class privilege remained untouched, the majority of citizens were pleased to settle for full employment, improved wages, a free medical service, much better social benefits, the provision of a decent home and a neighbourhood school of pleasing fashion. It was not the New Jerusalem, but, for many, it was a vast improvement on the pre-war decades.

The Labour Party broke all records with its national total of votes, something like 1.25 million more than the Conservatives, who, overall, enjoyed a small swing of just over 3 per cent, with a turnout of over 80 per cent, a result that, incidentally, shames modern voting in its degree of civic responsibility. Such was the stark choice between moving on or staying put that only 3 per cent of the votes cast were for candidates other than the two main parties.

There had been moves to redistribute seats from the depopulated city centres, although many claimed this was but a temporary phenomenon, pending rebuilding. This could have cost the Labour Party no less than forty seats, including nineteen in the London area alone. With 'masochistic honesty', Clement Attlee, upright as ever, advised 'it was the responsible thing to do at the time', but Herbert Morrison, that wily electioneering genius, was not prepared to be so generous and vetoed most of the proposals. The domestic performance of the government, based chiefly on a reduced overseas and military commitment, and the grateful young men saved from national service, had been strong, while the extrovert Prime Minister had busied himself cajoling and persuading the public, with his weather eye on clinging to some of the middle-class professional support of 1945. All in all, there was a wholesome majority of ninety-five for the second Morrison administration, where gloomy correspondents had prophesied it might have been just in single figures. Another step could be taken towards what the 1945 manifesto had termed 'the Socialist Commonwealth'.

With the old Labour guard retired, ill and dying, Herbert Morrison felt more at ease, surrounding himself with up and coming second-generation politicians he loved to describe as 'New Labour', like Hugh Gaitskell, Harold Wilson, Anthony Crosland, Jim Callaghan, Barbara Castle and others. They had five more years to run a more socially democratic regime now in times of increasing prosperity, still with an accent on a low-key foreign policy to which the public gradually adapted itself. The 1950 manifesto had called for the public ownership of a further swathe of mainly monopoly industries. Under Herbert Morrison's guidance, other mechanics were employed in these cases, drawing on the hybrid control of the iron and steel industry utilised in 1947, a scheme devised by him in preference to what nearly proved to be a disastrous 'board' plan. More crucial industries and services were brought under varied types of governmental regulation. Importantly for national financial management, the insurance industry was successfully 'mutualised' – Herbert Morrison was a devout co-operator, a lifelong customer of the Royal Arsenal Co-operative Society. Co-operative or 'mutualised' systems joined 'municipalisation' as other modes of public ownership.

A newly energised and confident Labour government also turned its reforming zeal on the citadels of privilege that had emerged from the war unharmed. The government built on

Lewis Silkin's 100 per cent land development levy to exert a more meaningful public oversight of land usage; the House of Lords, its veto power reduced from two years to one in the early Morrison days, soon became a merely advisory body, and the royal civil list was heavily cut, with some state duties transferred from the monarch to the Speaker of the House of Commons. Pay beds on NHS premises were gently phased out and medical students on state grants were, like the teacher trainees of the day, obliged to work five years in the state sector. The charitable status of fee-paying schools was abolished, an excise duty was placed on school fees, and state school pupils were given ever-increasing priority at state-funded universities and colleges. The comprehensive school agenda was fast tracked, and church and single-sex schools came under financial grant pressure to opt for less prejudicial modes.

All in all, it meant that a second phase of moderate – never revolutionary – reform in a more prosperous climate was negotiated. A more thorough-going social democratic state was founded. The consequent political story is well known to all. It was followed by a genuine 'Butskellite' ('Mr Butskell' was *The Economist*'s nickname for the left-of-centre Tory R. A. Butler) era of consolidation. Both Rab Butler and Hugh Gaitskell, the latter miraculously saved from a mysterious and near-fatal illness by swift action in one of Ellen Wilkinson's health centres, served confidently as Prime Minister. The nation was thus in much better shape to withstand the rigours of economic free-marketeering and the global oil-price crisis of the 1970s. The British republic ended the twentieth century serene at home and composed abroad, more a variegated and contented version of Denmark than a third-rate imitation of the USA.

There were, of course, many other ramifications of Herbert Morrison's coup at the expense of Clement Attlee, and the ensuing near decade of Morrrisonian government. An interesting cultural example is the government's refusal, unlike in many other countries, to sanction the development of commercial television in the early 1950s. Actually, the top brass of both leading political parties was opposed to so meretricious a proceeding, for, as Asa Briggs intimated in his classic history of the BBC, the corporation was liked by Labour because it was publicly owned and by the Tories because it was authoritarian. Only the mercurial Churchill, Leader of the Opposition, and a few young *arriviste* Conservative MPs were in favour. Long smarting from imagined BBC slights – 'for eleven years they kept me off the air' – he campaigned vigorously but vainly for the introduction of independent television.

There was much grief among the moneyed consortia keen to launch commercial broadcasting. There was particular sadness in the north-west, where mid-term plans had already reached the drawing board to present a soap opera of urban grittiness. Its working title was *Coronation Street*.

Prime Minister Gaitskell sends troops to Vietnam

Robert Taylor

It was always predictable that Hugh Gaitskell would turn out to be a controversial and divisive Prime Minister of the Labour government he formed after the party's comfortable general election victory in October 1964.

With an overall parliamentary majority of thirty-five, Labour returned to power after thirteen years in the political wilderness amidst widespread enthusiasm. Gaitskell was widely regarded as a man of high moral principle and an effective pragmatist, one who would transform Britain into a country of economic success, after years of relative decline, to become the envy of the world. His party's general election manifesto had set out a progressive agenda for government that seemed both credible and idealistic. Under Gaitskell's leadership the new government, so the manifesto argued, would rule 'with a sense of national purpose, start to create a dynamic, just and go-ahead Britain with the strength to stand on her own feet and to play a proper part in world affairs'. The 1964 manifesto went on to proclaim: 'We believe that such a New Britain is what the British people want and what the world wants. It is a goal that lies within our power to achieve.'

Of course, election manifestos are usually a triumph of hyperbole and false promises over reality. Labour's 1964 programme was no different, yet its bold rhetorical language captured the euphoric mood of the time. Gaitskell inspired millions of people beyond the Labour movement. He was even portrayed by more impressionable commentators as Britain's answer to John F. Kennedy, the glamorous American who had narrowly won his country's presidency four years earlier with his intoxicating dream of the New Frontier, and who had been assassinated in November 1963.

During much of his nearly nine years as Labour leader, beginning in December 1955, Gaitskell had found himself trying to make his quarrelsome party into one that was fit once more for government. He found himself struggling with a powerful left wing who fought against his revisionist reforming project that rejected state control of the commanding heights of the economy. By the time of his arrival in 10 Downing Street, Gaitskell appeared to have won the ideological debate within his party over the direction Labour policy was to take. The party had thrown off its so-called 'cloth cap' image and was now appealing more to the growing class of affluent, aspiring manual workers and their families who were becoming the key to electoral success in the marginal constituencies of south-east England, the suburbs of London and the industrial heartland of the west Midlands.

Gaitskell in opposition had failed to rewrite Clause Four of Labour's 1918 constitution, which committed the party to widespread public ownership of the means of production, distribution and exchange. The party's left were united with many of Gaitskell's trade union allies in resisting such a fundamental change to Clause Four. But in practice Gaitskell and his small group of like-minded revisionists shaped a political strategy that sought to combine the promise of economic growth with social justice, through state planning, redistributive taxation and a commitment to public sector expansion. The programme owed more to the thoughts of the contemporary American economist J. K. Galbraith than to any British socialist thinker.

By the autumn of 1964 Gaitskell towered over the political landscape. Many admirers convinced themselves he would become one of Britain's most successful twentieth-century peacetime Prime Ministers. Gaitskell was projected as a vigorous, intelligent, inspirational figure who would return Labour to the 'magnificent journey' on which it had first embarked between July 1945 and October 1951 under Clement Attlee.

Some of his close party colleagues took a more sceptical view of his abilities before he became Prime Minister. The then young centrist Anthony Wedgwood Benn noted in his diary in January 1963 that Gaitskell 'had a real civil servant's mind, very little imagination and hardly any understanding of how people worked'. 'His pernickety mind always manages to engineer a confrontation of principles which he then seeks to resolve by brute force,' he added. 'If you don't agree with him 100 per cent then he is not interested in you at all.' Denis Healey, a strong man on Labour's right-wing, took a similar view of his leader in the early 1960s. 'I am worried by a streak of intolerance in Gaitskell's nature,' he said. 'He tends to believe that no one can disagree with him unless they are either knaves or fools. He insists on arguing to a conclusion rather than to a decision.'

Despite such reservations from some of those close to Gaitskell he entered 10 Downing Street amidst expectations that his government would lead the country out of a period of relative decline and stagnation. But the realities of power in the 1960s proved to be harsh and unforgiving. There was to be no honeymoon; Gaitskell's government was characterised by endless internal conflict almost from its very beginning.

By the time of his sudden and unexpected death in October 1968 from a rare viral infection, Gaitskell had become a deeply unpopular and tragic figure as his divided party faced the real prospect of a severe defeat at the next general election, due within twelve months.

Gaitskell's government was not without substantial achievements. During his premiership, with his friend Roy Jenkins as Home Secretary, Britain became a more humane and civilised society. The government legalised homosexuality between consenting adults, abolished capital punishment, allowed abortion, introduced liberal divorce laws and put an end to most forms of censorship. Those measures were not left to Private Members' Bills. Gaitskell gave them top priority and provided government time for their passage through Parliament. The House of Lords was not abolished but it was reformed radically with an end to hereditary peerages and a further curbing of its powers.

The government's creation of the Open University, a new institution to provide long-distance learning opportunities for adult students via television, was also a Gaitskell triumph. Under his direction the government also introduced nation-wide comprehensive secondary education with the abolition of the grammar schools. This reform underlined his determination to champion a classless but also meritocratic education policy that sought to encourage upward social mobility and open up the system to all talents. There were even tentative moves to abolish fee-charging public schools.

In his early months as Prime Minister, Gaitskell also fought with some success to create a more generous and efficient welfare state. There was to be a massive improvement in the level of social benefits, particularly for old age pensioners, the sick and the poor. Britain had been falling behind other western European countries in its allocation of national resources to public spending. Now it looked as if Gaitskell would preside over a revolution in universal provision that would restore belief in the concept of social citizenship.

In opposition he had taken a brave stance against controls on immigration into Britain despite rising racial tensions. In government he was compelled to modify his position but what limitations were placed on the inward flow of non-white Commonwealth immigrants were balanced by a measure to outlaw forms of racial discrimination. Gaitskell also presided over measures to further female equality through an equal pay commitment, despite trade union indifference.

Before his arrival in 10 Downing Street Gaitskell was often portrayed as a technocratic mandarin in the Whitehall mould, more a senior civil servant than a Labour Party politician. The son of a colonial administrator, educated at the exclusive Dragon School in Oxford, Winchester and New College, Oxford, Gaitskell was an academic at London's University College in the 1930s. But this privileged background gave a misleading impression of his character. Gaitskell's first class honours degree was in the new subject of politics, philosophy and economics. He was much influenced by the polymath socialist academic G. D. H. Cole and mixed in left-wing circles. A year as an extramural lecturer on the Nottinghamshire coalfield brought him into personal contact with the proletariat. He always took a rather sentimental view of the manual working class.

Gaitskell could often be obstinate and rigid. He was driven as much by strong emotions as cool calculation. He was reluctant to back down under pressure. Even his friends believed he took an over-rational view of how to resolve political problems. But he also tended to lead from the front and despised the compromises and accommodations seen as necessary assets in presiding over a democratic party of the left. Gaitskell was often criticised for not broadening his power base in the party. It was said he relied too much for support and sympathy on a narrow right-wing cliqué of middle-class intellectuals who resided in or around the garden suburb of Hampstead.

But in the autumn of 1964 such doubts were brushed aside as Gaitskell formed the first Labour government in thirteen years. It was to prove a tough and often unrewarding responsibility. For most of his time as Prime Minister the country's deep intractable economic problems monopolised his attention. The legacy Gaitskell inherited from the Conservatives was horrendous with a huge balance of payments deficit, febrile international financial markets and a troubled sterling zone with the pound as a reserve currency.

In many respects Britain faced its severest economic crisis since 1951 when Labour had last been in government. As Chancellor of the Exchequer at that time, Gaitskell had seemed well equipped to do what needed to be done. A disciple of John Maynard Keynes, he had served as a senior civil servant during the war first at the newly formed Ministry of Economic Warfare and later at the Board of Trade. Gaitskell was a trained economist, the first to become a British Prime Minister. He believed strongly in demand management of the economy to prevent a return of mass unemployment on the scale of the 1930s and he endorsed the concept of a planned economy. Although he was never an uncritical enthusiast – as so many were in the Labour Party at that time – for the state ownership of the 'commanding heights' of the economy, he saw the strategic value of the public ownership of industry. In 1965 his government renationalised the iron and steel industry as promised. The state also extended its ownership into shipbuilding and the docks, with government financial support poured into the new technologies and science-based industries.

But in the macro management of the economy Gaitskell found it harder to make much progress. It is true that in running the Treasury during 1950–51 Gaitskell often seemed little more than the loyal exponent of Whitehall orthodoxies. During the early 1950s his apparently cross-party views on how to manage the economy seemed almost indistinguishable from those of Conservative Chancellor R. A. Butler. Norman Macrae at *The Economist* coined the term Butskellism to describe the post-war economic consensus that emerged. Gaitskell welcomed Harold Macmillan's creation of the National Economic Development Council in 1962. He also wanted to work through tripartite institutions of the state, employers and trade unions in dealing with the problems of low growth, poor productivity and lack of innovation that were said to be holding back the economy.

But after October 1964 there often seemed little time for his government to step back and establish long-term economic strategies. Gaitskell and his Cabinet were forced to take an early decision on whether or not to devalue sterling. A reduction in the parity of the pound would at least have provided Labour with some necessary breathing space to press ahead with their campaign promises of economic expansion and structural modernisation. But the new Prime Minister hesitated. As the man in charge of the 1949 devaluation he feared his government would lose much public and overseas confidence if it resorted to a similar manipulation of sterling that would be seen by many (wrongly) as a national humiliation. Like other Labour leaders before and since, Gaitskell was keen to reassure the markets and banks of Labour's respectability and competence in financial affairs.

At the last moment he had decided to appoint Harold Wilson as his Chancellor of the Exchequer. Wilson proved to be as cautious as Gaitskell in his views and his own position at the Treasury was strengthened by the Prime Minister's firm decision not to create a new separate Department of Economic Affairs. Instead the national debate over how to expand Britain's relatively stagnant economy was to be fought out inside the Treasury not between competing departments. Gaitskell made his close friend Tony Crosland Chief Secretary to the Treasury, alongside Wilson, with the specific task of implementing an expansionist programme, but only when the time was ripe.

Sadly that moment for planned expansion was never to arrive. During its first eighteen months Gaitskell's government fought to maintain an over-valued pound through the enforcement of increasingly austere policies of public expenditure cuts and restraints on consumer demand. Efforts to win voluntary co-operation from the trade unions, through the Trades Union Congress, in the moderation of wage claims and settlements failed as it had done in 1951. Inevitably Gaitskell found himself on an early collision course with his allies in the trade unions and in particular with Frank Cousins, General Secretary of the Transport and General Workers' Union who had turned down the offer of a Cabinet post.

When Chancellor himself in 1950–51, Gaitskell had urged the TUC and its affiliate members to back a voluntary national incomes policy that required severe wage restraint to reduce unit labour costs. Now as Prime Minister he was having to repeat his bleak message of austerity but to an expectant working-class audience that had been promised, and expected, a real and immediate improvement in their living standards through free collective bargaining. An early effort to meet some worker demands in a mini Budget in November 1964 had failed to satisfy expectations but it did enough to unsettle the suspicious and unsympathetic markets. The external pressures on sterling continued.

The abandonment of a voluntary approach to pay, with the introduction of a statutory incomes policy and the threat of penal sanctions against those who paid or received inflationary wage increases in the spring of 1965, made little difference. But it did alienate many workers and their families, who had voted Labour in October 1964 in the expectation of returning a Labour government that was committed to growth and an end to the old stop-go economic policies of the Conservatives. As a result, Labour began to lose a string of parliamentary by-elections from the winter of 1965 onwards.

By the spring of 1966 – after a damaging seamen's strike – Gaitskell decided his government faced no real alternative but to devalue sterling in order to revive the economy. The Cabinet was unanimous and the Labour Party relieved. At last it seemed that the government would be able to enjoy a greater degree of flexibility in its economic management and it provided some breathing space with the opportunity to return to the commitment to growth on which it had been elected.

Unfortunately this did not prove to be the case. For devaluation to succeed it needed more and not less restraint. It would involve recognition of greater electoral unpopularity and what Gaitskell described as two years of hard slog. There was no easy or quick fix for the British economy through devaluation.

Gaitskell's decision to devalue the pound and its aftermath provoked a full-scale political showdown between Gaitskell and Wilson. Relations between the two men had always proved difficult in the past. The Prime Minister had not forgiven Wilson's challenge to his leadership in November 1960 after he narrowly lost the support of the Scarborough Party conference over unilateral nuclear disarmament. Wilson himself had been no supporter of banning the British Bomb but he had believed he was better able than Gaitskell to keep the Labour Party united over the defence issue. Gaitskell had won that battle and had sought to placate Wilson by making him Chancellor. As Prime Minister he had restrained himself for a long time from incessant interference in the Treasury. Now Gaitskell decided after devaluation to replace Wilson with Crosland to push ahead with a growth strategy.

Crosland's appointment as Chancellor incensed the left. The Cabinet resignations of Wilson, Richard Crossman and Barbara Castle rekindled the old party divisions of the 1950s. At the same time the post-devaluation economy deteriorated. Rising unemployment and a worsening inflation rate were accompanied by a sudden outbreak of rank and file trade union militancy. The country's two largest trade unions elected men of the left as their general secretaries – Jack Jones and Hugh Scanlon respectively. They openly challenged Gaitskell's economic strategy and called on his government to introduce a more Socialist programme. Unofficial strikes crippled key industries like engineering, auto production and ship building, while low-paid public service workers grew restive. Gaitskell began to contemplate legislation to curb industrial disruption and make trade unions more efficient, accountable and democratic. But for all his reputation for decisiveness he held back from trying to force through what many believed was necessary trade union reform.

It was becoming increasingly clear that Gaitskell had lost the backing of an important section of the Parliamentary Labour Party. Some MPs began to wonder whether life would be easier if a more emollient figure like Wilson replaced him as Prime Minister, although this did not bring an immediate leadership challenge.

But by the summer of 1968 the government's growing troubles were not confined to economic affairs. Gaitskell had always been an unswerving champion of Britain's so-called 'special relationship' with the United States. Although he did not visit the country for the first time until after the Second World War, he adored the exclusive social world of the east coast liberal intellectuals like Arthur Schlesinger, J. K. Galbraith and other advisers who had belonged to President Kennedy's Camelot and continued to serve under President Lyndon Johnson. Gaitskell also shared the tough anti-communism of Dean Acheson and George Kennan. He was a committed enthusiast of NATO and SEATO and British military involvement in the Korean War. He had even been ready to defy Aneurin Bevan's resistance to the imposition of charges on spectacles and teeth in early 1951, regarded as necessary by the Treasury to raise public money to contribute to the cost of the country's spiralling arms burden. Gaitskell did not share the American Manichean view of the Cold War and calls for a rollback of Soviet Communism in Europe by force if necessary. He believed in containment, détente, peaceful coexistence and multilateral diplomacy. But he never held any sentimental view of Soviet intentions. In 1960–61 he had stood up successfully to his party's left and supporters in the Campaign for Nuclear Disarmament who had wanted a non-nuclear defence policy. But he was never convinced that Britain should renounce its own nuclear independence. In October 1964 Gaitskell made it clear that Britain would continue to provide facilities for American nuclear bases and he was keen to uphold the country's own nuclear deterrent.

Gaitskell was a patriot as well as a socialist but he continued to admire the United States and its outlook on the world as Prime Minister. Within a few months of entering 10 Downing

Street his loyalty to Washington was put to the test. Gaitskell came under unrelenting pressure from President Johnson to dispatch a token task force of British troops to assist the Americans in their escalating war against Communist insurgency in South Vietnam.

It was not an easy request to reject or accept. But Gaitskell was not only an uncritical admirer of US foreign policy; he was also emotionally committed to the defence of the British Commonwealth. He was influenced over Vietnam by the view emanating from Australia, Singapore and Malaysia that British power and influence in south-east Asia required military involvement in South Vietnam. Additionally, British troops were engaged in dealing with Communist insurgents in Borneo and the country had just completed a successful campaign against Communists in Malaya. The deployment of troops from those war zones to neighbouring South Vietnam made strategic sense to Gaitskell. Moreover it was widely believed that Britain's successful counter terrorist tactics in Malaya could achieve similar results in Indo-China. Gaitskell agreed to Johnson's request early in 1966.

It was to prove a fateful and catastrophic decision. Gaitskell was always a stubborn man and he had come to believe British military intervention in South Vietnam was the right thing to do. With firm Atlanticists Denis Healey at the Foreign Office and George Brown at Defence, along with Jenkins and Crosland, the Prime Minister was well supported in backing the Americans. But Gaitskell's decision brought an inevitable disaffection among left-wing members of the Parliamentary Labour Party and eventual resignations from the Cabinet. It also gave a powerful boost to the growing protest movement in Britain as many thousands took to the streets in a campaign of marches and civil disobedience.

Opposition grew dramatically through 1966 and 1967 as Britain's mounting toll of dead and wounded soldiers were brought back from the battlefields of Vietnam. Inevitably as the allied cause failed to achieve any semblance of victory, the demand for ever more British troops to be thrown into the quagmire grew increasingly intense. The Communist Vietcong's Tet offensive of January 1968 gave a huge impetus to the already massive anti-war movement on both sides of the Atlantic.

Gaitskell had hoped to secure influence in Washington as a result of sending British troops to South Vietnam. He favoured a multilateral negotiated settlement to end the war and often found himself in conflict with President Johnson over tactics as the Americans resorted to chemical warfare and military methods that were seen by many observers as criminal.

In fact, Britain's military involvement in the conflict had failed to make much impact. Public opinion was revolted by the mounting civilian casualties caused by indiscriminate American bombing. As the next British general election neared, the Prime Minister began to look at ways of extricating the country's forces from the horrors of South Vietnam through a phased military withdrawal. There were growing demands for a public inquiry into how and why the country had gone to war in support of the United States and in no obvious national interest. The Conservative opposition under its anti-American leader Edward Heath claimed that if he was elected he would bring an immediate end to British military involvement by setting a date for a final withdrawal. His opposition paralleled the stance of Republican front-runner Richard Nixon in the United States. The pressures were clearly building up on Gaitskell to act decisively over Vietnam by the summer of 1968.

For a short time British military backing for the US had brought some assistance to the country's economy. President

Johnson had not needed to threaten Gaitskell's government with hostile economic countermeasures if it did not provide him with support. On the contrary, he bullied the US Treasury, the World Bank and the International Monetary Fund to assist Britain to recover from its post-devaluation economic woes. There had been no formalised deal that linked US support for sterling on international markets to British troop deployment in Vietnam. But an implied understanding was apparent. By 1968, however, this was becoming increasingly difficult to sustain in the face of Britain's underlying economic weaknesses and the growing awareness in a divided America that its own massive involvement in Vietnam could no longer run in parallel with huge public spending on building Johnson's Great Society.

By the spring of 1968 other issues were also crowding their way onto Gaitskell's troubled agenda. After thirty years of relative peace and stability, Northern Ireland was becoming an unexpected cause for official concern with the rise of the civil rights movement and its threat to Unionist dominance. In southern Rhodesia the right-wing white settlers led by Ian Smith had declared unilateral independence from Britain. As a liberal imperialist Gaitskell had been a firm champion of decolonisation in Africa and his threats of military intervention had deterred Smith from going ahead with UDI. But now Smith called Gaitskell's bluff at a time when the Prime Minister lacked the means for decisive intervention. Gaitskell applied economic sanctions and moved British troops into neighbouring Zambia. But he was concerned apartheid South Africa would intervene in support of Smith's illegal regime and stretch Britain to breaking point. Moreover, public opinion was not in favour of overthrowing Smith and the white settlers. Gaitskell tried to find a diplomatic way out of the Rhodesia crisis but by the time his premiership ended little progress had been made.

On one vexatious issue, however, Gaitskell appeared to stand firm. He did not change his mind about the wisdom of applying for Britain to join the European Economic Community. During the 1966 devaluation crisis and its aftermath a serious debate took place inside the Cabinet and beyond on whether Britain should seek a new relationship with western Europe through an application to join the EEC. In the autumn of 1962 Gaitskell had rejected the UK's first membership bid to the chagrin of his right-wing Labour friends like Jenkins and Crosland. Four years later he was of the same opinion. He did not believe the way forward to achieve British economic success lay through full participation in the EEC. Furthermore he reasoned it made little sense to re-examine UK membership as long as France was ruled by President de Gaulle, who feared Britain would be a threat to the future development of a united Europe based on the Franco–German alliance. The Conservatives under Heath were now committed to EEC entry.

By the autumn of 1968 Gaitskell was faced by horrendous difficulties at home and abroad. But observers were not convinced his government was in terminal decline. It was still seen as possible that he could stage a recovery, mainly because Heath's Conservatives were in disarray. But in a few short weeks Gaitskell was compelled to resign as Prime Minister.

What triggered his tragic downfall? There seemed to be no obvious answer at the time beyond concern over his health. But the writer Ian Fleming's decision to sue his Tory hostess wife Ann for divorce and name Gaitskell as co-respondent proved decisive.

There were many rumours of who encouraged Fleming to take such drastic action. After all, Ann Fleming had openly been Gaitskell's mistress for at least twelve years in what had been an open marriage on both sides. Gaitskell's close friends had always feared his exposure and were troubled by the liaison. Some of them pointed the finger inevitably at Wilson and particularly his scurrilous aide George Wigg. Certainly Wilson's decisive election as the new party leader and Prime Minister in October 1968 indicated he was the main beneficiary of Gaitskell's downfall. His arrival at 10 Downing Street led to a dramatic improvement in Labour's poll ratings and within six months he called a general election which he went on to win.

But it was more likely that the move against Gaitskell originated in Conservative circles frequented by Ann Fleming. Many of them had always hated him as a class traitor. They also began to think Labour under his leadership might win the next general election, which was due by October 1969 at the latest, despite all the government's difficulties. This would strengthen Labour's claim that they had become the natural party of government. There was also a suggestion that the intelligence services were behind Fleming's move.

Gaitskell's open affair with a Tory hostess reflected what most of his friends regarded as the strong streak of Bohemian recklessness that had characterised the way he had behaved for a long time. But it also betrayed his tragic flaw. It was difficult to separate his public life from his private life in the way David Lloyd George had done as Prime Minister with his liaison with Frances Stevenson. The revelation of Gaitskell's adultery had nearly burst into the public gaze during the 1963 Profumo affair which had rocked Macmillan's Conservative government. The exposure that the War Secretary had been sleeping with a young woman (Christine Keeler – who had also been going to bed with the naval attaché at the Soviet embassy) was widely seen as a decisive blow to Macmillan's continuation as Prime Minister. In the great moral hysteria of the time the emotional Tory chairman Lord Hailsham had fulminated on television about adulterers on the Labour front bench but stopped short of naming Gaitskell. But Gaitskell's friends were well aware of the dangers. Britain may have become a more tolerant society in the swinging sixties but they doubted Gaitskell could have survived the exposure of his affair with Ann Fleming.

In the autumn of 1968 the 61-year-old Gaitskell was exhausted. The threat of scandal over his private life made him decide to resign. In fact, it was soon clear that he was seriously ill. Within a few weeks he collapsed and died shortly afterwards of a rare virus. There was a terrible suspicion that Soviet intelligence had been responsible for poisoning him, but it was never proved.

Gaitskell's political life had ended in personal tragedy. The hopes of October 1964 remained unfulfilled. But the problems his government faced were too deep rooted and complex for any one person to resolve successfully. After his death the economic troubles of the country worsened as industrial militancy grew, unemployment soared and wage inflation threatened to increase out of control. In the 1970s Britain, with other Western capitalist countries, fell into the most serious crisis since the end of the war. As a result the post-war social settlement began to collapse. It was openly questioned whether the kind of social democratic politics personified by Gaitskell would survive.

The Labour Party grew more factious and it plunged into internecine war over its future. The right wing, which had drawn inspiration from Gaitskell, failed to build on his legacy. The emergent left capitalised on the frustrations and disappointments experienced during his government.

Gaitskell was increasingly seen as the last hope of a democratic socialism that had come to dominate the Labour Party in the 1930s and reached its zenith under Attlee after 1945. He tried to bring a coherence and inspiration to his centre-left government but the remorseless sweep of external events undermined his efforts. It was doubted whether Britain was governable any longer through the application of the principles that had dominated its political life for the quarter century after 1945.

But Gaitskell's admirers questioned this opinion. They believed that the record of his government had pointed to a better way. Their views were based more on wishful thinking than a hard-headed recognition of the facts. Nobody – not even an intelligent and forceful figure like Gaitskell – could defy the logic of events. His government had sought to reverse the trends of relative national decline through its own exertions. But Britain was vulnerable to the vagaries of the international economy, the retreat from Empire, a growing revolt at home against high taxes, collectivism and high public spending.

Gaitskell came to recognise those difficulties as Prime Minister but he was unable to do much about them. He found himself the victim of his own party's ideological limitations and the perilous conditions of an overstretched economy. After his death his reputation grew through myths and legends propagated by faithful Gaitskellites like Jenkins and Crosland. His reputation grew as his successors failed. But his achievements were oversold.

Prime Minister Butler and the Democratic Centralist Party

Chris Proctor

Earlier this year David Miliband became leader of the UK's Democratic Centralist Party – the party which, with the exception of the Socialist Party government of 1979, has now ruled Britain for more than half a century. In his acceptance speech David spoke movingly of the party's iconic founder, Rab Butler, the man who became Prime Minister in 1957 after the resignation of the Conservative Anthony Eden.

'Under my leadership I urge the DCP to continue to engage with the big issues facing Britain with an openness, a freshness, a vivacity unlike anything it has seen since Rab's day,' Mr Miliband said. 'We need to constantly remodel ourselves – in the way Rab urged after the Conservatives lost the 1945 general election.'

As we approach the sixtieth anniversary of Rab's emergence as Prime Minister, it is a good time to reassess the central role he played in the making of modern Britain.

Rab's accession to the premiership was a surprise to many. He was felt to lack the driving ambition that politicians need to reach the summit. Rab had long been suspected of a lack of ruthlessness. In many other professions this would be a positive, but not in politics. He had been a thinker, a man concerned with the 'art of the possible', rather than a player, anxious for power. Yet when it became obvious that Eden would fall, Rab showed a single-minded drive that led him to Downing Street. How did this 'new Rab' emerge?

For one thing, his wife, Sydney, died in 1954. Rab could see her slip away a little more each day as the cancer ate into her body. He often said she provided his 'astringent spurs', driving him on to new levels not simply by persuasion but by providing him with the security and self-regard that he needed to seek high office. It was almost that he felt he needed to secure the premiership for her sake and for her memory. In the trying times of her illness he devoted himself to politics in a way that he never had before. It was only after he left the House to take up the job of Master of Trinity College, Cambridge that he married Mollie Courtauld, widow of the Artic explorer.

Was there also a hint that Rab had a real sense of his destiny in 1957? Certainly, according to all who knew him, he spoke more than ever about Robert Peel. He was an authority on Peel, having taken an almost obsessive interest in the nineteenth-century politician during his student days. A century and a half later the close parallels with his contemporary situation preyed on Rab's mind.

Peel had seen the need for radical political change after the ravages of the Napoleonic wars. He recognised that the great war leader, Wellington rather than Churchill, had served his time. He saw the need for a complete change in his party's outdated policies. Old values and attitudes needed to be relaxed, others rejected outright. As Rab said, 'We feel the breeze of change moving into a wind.'

No one has ever suggested that Rab set out to cause a schism in the old Conservative party of the scale that emerged, but equally his commitment to change was unequivocal. It was not inevitable that Rab's leadership would lead to the desperate fight with the reactionaries that emerged, but in retrospect it was likely. There was no meeting of minds between the reactionaries and those who, while wanting to conserve what was best of what existed, did not have their minds set against reform. Just as huge swathes of Peel's party could not be reconciled to his Tamworth Manifesto – with its welcome for the 1832 Reform Act, a review of civil and ecclesiastical institutions and the correction of popular grievances – so Rab's outlook and history could not be accepted by the 'shire' Conservatives of his day. Unquestionably Rab saw parallels between his policy reviews, the Charters for which he was responsible, and Peel's Manifesto.

All these years later it seems strange to think of Rab as a Conservative, or that the 'Tories', as they were known, were once such a central part of the British political system. Yet his first stint as Prime Minister was under Conservative colours. Even more surprising to a younger generation is the fact that the only man who seriously challenged Rab for the leadership was the disgraced politician Harold Macmillan.

Macmillan was Chancellor in the Eden government during the 'Macmillan Crisis' of 1956. At the time he was seen as a possible challenger to Rab, but all that came to grief when his role in the 'Suez Affair' was uncovered. Looking back, the situation borders on the incredible.

Unknown to the majority of the Cabinet, Macmillan had plotted with the security forces of the Israeli government to provoke conditions for a British war with Egypt. The plan was for the Israelis to invade Egypt, at which point an Anglo-French army would arrive like some latter-day US cavalry loosely disguised as 'peacekeepers'. The British troops would then occupy the Suez Canal in order to prevent President Nasser of Egypt from taking it over.

Even more remarkable, Macmillan had plans to depose the democratically elected Nasser and impose a British puppet in a sovereign state. As Rab said at the time, 'It was a project that can only be seen as underhand, adventurist and morally repugnant.' The exact role of Rab in publicly unmasking Macmillan's plotting remains obscure, but he certainly shared the details with a group of Tory backbenchers – the Progress Trust – and must have known such explosive material would find its way into the public arena. It is perhaps more likely that Rab's protégé and later Chancellor, Edward Heath, was more active in this regard. But someone ensured that Macmillan's role was made public and his career was shredded.

When Macmillan's central role in the planning was revealed, he lost not only the backing of his Conservative allies, but also, and perhaps more importantly for his career, that of the press – and in particular his close associate Lord Beaverbrook.

By 1957 Beaverbrook had turned the *Daily Express* into the most widely read newspaper in the world, founded the *Sunday Express* and purchased the *Evening Standard*. The extent of the power of his media empire – and his anger against the folly of his former protégé – became gruesomely clear when the Beaverbrook newspapers began to reveal, first in innuendo and then in graphic detail, the unorthodox relationship between Macmillan, his wife Dorothy and the Tory MP Robert Boothby. It had all the elements of a top-class gutter-raking tale for the less discriminating of Fleet Street's finest. In addition to details of the unusual relationship between Mr Macmillan and his wife, suggestions, now largely dismissed as speculative, were made concerning the bisexual Mr Boothby and the politician. They were given credence when witnesses including J. B. S. Haldane claimed that buggery was the reason for Macmillan's abrupt departure from Eton before taking his examinations.

This was followed by allegations that the police failed to investigate the death of Lady Dorothy Macmillan's brother, Edward Cavendish, the tenth Duke of Devonshire. Cavendish died in the company of suspected serial killer Dr John Bodkin Adams, who then signed a death certificate saying the Duke died naturally. The deluge continued with rumours that Boothby was the father of Sarah Macmillan. Some of this resulted from the widely-reported tale that when a dancing partner apologised profusely for treading on her toes, especially because of who her father was, she exclaimed, 'You're dancing with the most famous bastard in England. Everyone knows I'm Bob Boothby's daughter.'

Further inside information, which would certainly have been known to Butler and Heath, revealed that all Macmillan's offspring suffered from alcoholism. He was dead in the water, and Rab was unchallenged as the senior political figures of his day. Macmillan dropped to the backbenches before resigning his Bromley seat and then retiring to continue his life-long mission of murdering grouse.

Anthony Eden, the Prime Minister of the day, was not up to his duties. During the 'Macmillan Crisis' he cracked, simply absconding to a Caribbean island, leaving the British army in Egypt, the Conservative Party in turmoil and the government in Rab's care. When it was evident that Macmillan's role in Suez would be exposed, the party turned to Butler to save it from the savaging at the polls it clearly deserved. The Queen, bizarrely, and in fact unconstitutionally, called Churchill in to seek his advice. The excuse was that Eden was out of the county, but there were unquestionably other methods of communication, among them the telephone. But for whatever reason, Churchill was wheeled down to the Palace.

The details of the subsequent conversation will probably

never be revealed. Rumours abound that he sought to grasp power once again for himself, but that this was politely not conceded. One unnamed courtier is reported as hearing the war leader emerging from his audience with a face like thunder, muttering malevolently, 'then it will have to be that bloody Butler'.

An inauspicious start, perhaps, but it transpired to be a potent turning point for British politics and for his party. Rab's swift, decisive and uncharacteristically robust actions saved the Conservative Party from losing the 1959 election. In what became known as the 'night of the long knives', he kissed the hands of the Queen, became the Prime Minister – and promptly dismissed half his Cabinet.

It appeared that there was no way the Conservatives could pull off the election of 1959, so badly scarred was the country by the Suez invasion. Yet Rab, at this single stroke, reasserted the moral supremacy of his party, restored faith in politics in the country and began the rift in the Tory Party that would lead to the creation of the Democratic Centralist Party (DCP).

'The British people deserve a government of moral integrity,' Rab told the House of Commons the first time he addressed them as Prime Minister. 'They have not been given it. A number of members of Mr Eden's government showed themselves not up to this task. That has been remedied. Now we will get on with the business of government.'

And that is what he did, to the extent that the Conservatives held onto power until the great schism of the coming decade and the formation of the DCP.

Rab's first act was to withdraw British troops from the Suez Canal zone. 'You call this a retreat?' he demanded in the Commons debate. 'I say it is an advance. An advance for Britain's position in the eyes of the world. A great step forward for our relations with all the nations of the Middle East. Our British troops are not going to make war in Egypt as my predecessors plotted. They are going to the Sudan to make peace.'

The transfer of the troops to act as peacekeepers between the warring north and south of Sudan was short-lived and not successful, but at the time it was a political masterstroke. It was difficult for any opposition to be raised to a peacekeeping role in a land with such strong ties to the UK.

At the same time he sent his new Foreign Secretary, the youthful Edward Heath, to speak face to face with Nasser. Heath's brief, overwhelmingly the work of Rab, was to establish good relations between the two countries and to come to an agreement based on (a) secure guarantees of international use of the Canal through international law – in effect through the United Nations, (b) compensation for the mostly British and French shareholders, (c) UK contracts for the building of the Aswan Dam and (d) a state visit to the UK for the Egyptian leader.

Rab flew to the United Nations and explained exactly what he was seeking to achieve. He held frank meetings with Egyptian representatives, mirroring Heath's work in Cairo. The culmination of this charm offensive was Butler's highly staged 'surprise' visit to Nasser on his way back from the UN. Within days of assuming the premiership, Rab had cut the bonds of the past, both in terms of government and of party.

In a statement even more remarkable in hindsight, Rab said that good relations with, and between, Egypt and Israel would be central to maintaining world peace in the future. He said, 'By helping to alleviate a cycle of flood and famine in Egypt, and by supporting its democratically elected leaders, we will assist that country's stability, confidence and prosperity. This will create the optimum conditions for talks between Egypt and Israel to be fruitful and successful.'

Rab's handling of the end of the Suez affair, almost incredibly, led to an increase in support for the Conservatives and a vast improvement in the UK's standing in international relations. Harold Wilson was later to call it 'a political masterstroke' in his memoirs. 'We found all our attacks were aimed at a Tory leadership that had disappeared,' he said.

However, while this series of bold political strokes won favour from the electorate and the grudging support of both the Labour and Liberal parties, it became the central reason for a rift in the old Conservative Party that had, in effect, been bubbling since consensus politics had emerged during and after the Second World War. On the one side was Rab and his 'modern conservatism', on the other was the old Tory right, solely interested in maintaining its privileged position, with whom Rab had battled for a decade. In the end, the right simply upped sticks and left.

To many of the 'shire Tories', Rab was little else than a traitor, a serial offender against Tory principles – and had been from the start. They always suspected, with justification, his relaxed attitude to the end of empire. Many of his party felt the remnants of empire had a duty to be grateful, while others entertained a sense of ownership of those areas coloured red on their globes. To give them away meant accepting that Great Britain, and its conquering world war heroes, were relegated to the second division of global nations. It was too much to take, especially from men like Gandhi, Churchill's 'half naked fakir'.

Rab made little secret of his impatience with such views. He wrote that he was 'out of sympathy with Conservative principles' and that delegates to the party conference 'would have been a credit to the zoo'. He saw 'no ray of enlightenment'. At least there was this sense of balance: that he was as disillusioned with them as they were with him.

The war element bore a grudge against him because of his advocacy of appeasement before the Second World War. Rab had been high-profile in these debates as a junior foreign office minister while the Foreign Secretary, Lord Halifax, was confined to the Lords. Even worse, in their eyes, he did not advocate it because it would give the country time to re-arm, but because he genuinely believed it to be the best course of action. He told the Commons in October 1939, 'war settles nothing'– a message the right would never forget. They saw him as weak, even traitorous, at a time that the country was awash with desire for wartime sacrifice and noble achievement.

Then there were his education reforms – the famous 1944 Education Act. Had he set out to alienate every strata of the right he could not have done a better job. He estranged himself from Christians, churchmen and believers of all denominations by reversing the system whereby the state supplemented church education. He became suspect in the eyes of the extreme right as he championed industrial and technical training, and admitted his disillusion with his colleagues when he said, 'I find in education that much of the drive towards a vaguely progressive future comes from Labour.' Then came the rift with the public schoolboys, the backbone of the Tory right, when he proposed to 'examine the position of public schools'. He noted with commendable understatement that this 'may easily raise widespread controversy'. The 'may' was clearly superfluous. But it did show that Rab was ready for the rift even before he became Prime Minister. He knew the public schools were the basis of privilege in the country and belonged exclusively to the Tory hierarchy. The playing fields of Eton were the natural place for the leaders of the country to be nurtured. And they felt they were being challenged on their own turf.

The right began to organise around Lord Salisbury's 'Watching Committee' and the Monday Club of the Commons. And as the protests became louder and more frequent, Rab began to move the goalposts again. He began the famous talks with the Liberals that led to the electoral pact of 1964 and the subsequent landslide victory for the anti-left alliance that was to become the Democratic Centralist Party.

Rab found his discussions with the Liberals an easy exercise. After all he had spoken to them about an electoral pact for the 1951 elections. In June of that year he drew up an 'Overlap Prospectus of Principles' which he discussed with Lady Violet Bonham Carter. She confirmed in a letter to him that the agenda included 'principles with which both parties might find themselves in general agreement'. The initiative floundered on electoral reform, but Rab felt able to 'stress how much closer I think we have got despite the obvious setbacks'.

By the 1960s the Liberals were ready to talk of formal amalgamation within a new party because their post-war experiences had made them nervous about their future. Even when they were successful, they failed. They had recovered from the nadir of 1951 to the extent that by 1962, following their capture of the traditionally Conservative seat of Orpington, an opinion poll showed them ahead of all their rivals with support of 33.7 per cent. They calculated, rightly, that if they added the Butler wing of the Conservative party, the combination would be irrepressible. Together they provided a single party that represented the vast majority of the ambitions of the post-war consensus.

The effect on both the left and right of British politics was enormous. Labour, defeated and humiliated, began to tear themselves apart. When Wilson led the right of the party into the Democratic Centralist Party in 1960, the rump was suddenly vulnerable to other pressures – especially from the Communist Party of Great Britain (CPGB).

Wilson's decision was partly due to his feeling of impotence within the Labour Party, which, as he said, 'enjoyed a bloodbath at the seaside each summer as it paraded its internal hatreds to the nation'. It is true that the debates of the late 1950s and early 1960s were fractious and often ugly. As he said at his final Labour conference, 'We will either cease to be the party of protest and become a party of government – or we are all wasting our time.' When he was secretly offered the succession to Rab in the new party, his mind was made up. Wilson saw no future in slogging out the same battle each year with his left wing and deeply resented the favours, and finance, that left him in debt to the new active trade unionism of Jack Jones and Hugh Scanlon who were in turn being, as far as Wilson was concerned, 'led by the nose by Moscow'.

The CPGB had failed in bids to affiliate to Labour in 1935, '43 and '46. The sudden exodus of a third of the party provided new opportunities for the Communists. While the CPGB had not enjoyed electoral success, it remained highly significant in the Labour movement. At the height of its influence from the war years to 1956, it moulded many of the ideas of the Labour left, and had disproportionately high representation in the unions, especially the mineworkers, electricians and engineers. The eventual merger of the remainder of Labour and the CPGB into the British Socialist Party provided a left alternative in Britain, and also led to electoral disaster.

The right who left the Conservative Party at the same time drifted until it eventually evolved into the National Front, effectively becoming the natural heirs of Mosley's fascists.

However, the party's involvement, and particularly that of Enoch Powell, in the race riots first in Nottingham and Notting Hill and eventually reaching just about every major city, effectively ended the Front as an electoral force. It was swiftly abandoned by the old Tories, whose interests were the defence of privilege, the birch and the re-establishment of their 'natural order'. They did not identify with the radicalism of the Powellites and recoiled in horror at the violence and rioting inspired by 'their' party. They were 'shire Tories', not fascists.

Closer links between the UK and Europe led to Britain becoming a founder member of the European Common Market and Union. The leading position of the UK on the European scene is one of Rab's greatest legacies.

His relationship with de Gaulle was central to the way this developed. As Rab remembered later, 'I became almost a friend of de Gaulle. She was a charming woman.' It was a typical Butler joke, containing much truth. With his First from Oxford in French, and his calm and assured manner, he charmed Mme de Gaulle, a practical and down-to-earth woman who lived in the shadow of the tall General. Little did Rab know at the time how this relationship would serve his cause. The General, whose bluster and arrogance Rab found difficult to bear, was always aware of slights to his rather ordinary partner, be they real or imaginary. She was not a great thinker or talker and de Galle protected and watched over her with great care. Rab's obvious careful and polite manner with her did as much to establish the UK's place at the European table as any of Heath's diplomatic manoeuvres. Heath later gave a rather different version of why Rab and Mme de Gaulle had got along together. 'Rab spoke a lot to Madame because he couldn't stand talking to the General,' he said. But regardless of the motives, the UK gradually became not just a participant in Europe, but a leader.

The choice for Britain, it was said at the time, was 'America or Europe'. Rab's logical mind (and as he said 'understanding of geography') led him in the direction of the latter. When he signed the two Treaties of Rome on 25 March 1957 he was committed entirely to the formation of the European Economic Community but less enthusiastic about the establishment of the European Atomic Energy Community. He was always ambivalent about nuclear power and had a loathing of nuclear arms.

As an intellectual, he had a fear and hatred of war and he never felt any great need for the UK to have an independent nuclear deterrent. He felt it had little electoral importance and was not prepared to pay the price of 'bowing and scraping' to the United States in order to secure it. Neither could Rab see any logic in the US refusal to share its nuclear research with France. 'They will share it with Europe, or Europe will make its own arrangements,' he said.

He was never anti-American, but he felt little genuine warmth for the country. He had scant intellectual respect for what he famously, after the Bay of Pigs invasion, called a 'politically emerging nation with a simple two-party system – a conservative party called the Republicans and ... another conservative party called the Democrats'. Some American commentators dismissed Rab as a 'British snob' and in some ways, although they were essentially wrong, this does contain some truth. Perhaps Rab's relations with John F. Kennedy encapsulate the true position, more of bewilderment than antagonism.

Rab thought Kennedy a strange creature and, as with Eden, found he could not treat him seriously. At the first meeting between the pair in America Kennedy is supposed to have asked Rab where he 'got his money'. To Rab, this was a question that was never asked: 'one simply had money, or one did not.' So Rab outlined generations of Butler diplomatic and state service, academics and administrators, a casual account of British aristocratic life, then said: 'And on what is the Kennedy dynasty founded?' Kennedy was, for once, silent. Bootleg whiskey was clearly not a suitable response even if it happened to be the truth.

There is also the story of Kennedy confiding in Rab that 'if I don't have sex for three days I get a headache. Do you find that?' The donnish Prime Minister Butler considered for a moment before replying. 'No,' he said. 'I get a headache after sex, Mr President. And I have been mercifully free of that ailment since the death of my wife.'

Undoubtedly the formal rather than close links with the United States, allied with Rab's obvious desire to cease the 'anachronisms of empire', made entry onto the European stage a great deal easier than it could otherwise have been, but it also raised some difficult issues which are still to be resolved. He posed it in these terms, 'The age of imperialism is over in Africa and in India. In that process, Britain has lost an empire and needs to find a new role.' He recognised, as the country did not, that Britain was no longer a world power; the difference was that Rab was content with the situation. 'It is how history works,' he said. 'Events, dear boy. Events.'

In a paper he wrote on the Dutch Empire when he later returned to academic life, he said the Dutch had taken three hundred years to accept the fact that they were no longer a great power and that he thought they were perhaps one-third of the way to reconciling themselves to that fact. 'The tragedy for the UK,' he said, 'is that we do not have that nation's gift of adapting to change so speedily.'

Although the UK was represented at most of the set-piece ritualistic meetings to discuss nuclear disarmament, privately they never enthused him for two reasons. First, he thought the reality of politics was that progress was impossible: there was insufficient trust between the United States and the Soviets for either to voluntarily disarm. He lost interest in the unachievable, believing in the art of the possible. And secondly, he believed that discussions over defence should be conducted by Europe rather than its constituent parts. 'Was that not why we fought two wars?' he asked rhetorically. 'So that Europe would not be divided militarily again?'

Rab's attitudes were far too progressive to be aired publicly, but he did begin a process for preparing future politicians to face up to a more limited role for the UK in line with its size, population and income. As he wrote in his memoirs, 'It must be faced, and better sooner than later. Our party must lead, because radicals and revolutionaries cannot deliver great change.'

Rab resigned as Prime Minister in 1962 at the age of sixty, and took up his position as Master of Trinity College. He did so for both political and personal reasons. He felt his energy for the task diminishing and believed it was time to give others a chance. He had also recently re-married, to Mollie, a former friend of his first wife, Sydney, and another member of the Courtauld family. He left politics with little regret. 'Politics is the art of the possible, but it is also a grubby affair at times,' he said.

There was more grubbiness to come, but Rab had happily moved on by then. Wilson, much more suited to the cut and thrust, proved an able successor. His relations with the media were much more cultivated and it was the press rather than the security services that tipped him off about the emerging Profumo scandal.

The story is that Beaverbrook held the story back until Wilson had called and won the 1963 election. Within days, in almost a mirror of the actions taken by Rab back in 1951, there was a major reshuffle, in which Jeremy Thorpe became Chancellor and Profumo was dropped from government. The subsequent scandal was undoubtedly a blow, but the worst effects on the Democratic Centralist Party were deflected.

The one assurance that was not delivered in the formation of the DCP was that the Liberal Jeremy Thorpe would succeed Wilson in 1976. Thorpe's career ended with another first-rate scandal that featured bitten sheets, shot dogs and Devon moors. That was when Edward Heath finally got his reward for decades of loyalty. Heath, of course, served as Prime Minister until he stepped down to become the first President of the European Union.

Prime Minister George Brown and Charles de Gaulle

Paul Routledge

George Brown owed his climb to the premiership to an enormous stroke of good fortune. His secret on-off relationship with Christine Keeler, while well known to the security services, was never revealed in salacious media coverage of the Profumo Affair. So, following the tragic death of Hugh Gaitskell he was able to offer himself as the moderate, trustworthy candidate for the Labour Party leadership. By contrast, his rival Harold Wilson, for whom he confessed a 'pestilential hatred and contempt', was portrayed as a shifty leftist, probably with clandestine Soviet sympathies.

This was a gross misrepresentation. Brown ('my patriotic George', as he liked Keeler to call him) was well aware of his mistress's links with Russian embassy spook Eugene Ivanov. It could have been an even bigger scandal. But the British establishment wanted Brown. On the brink of a strategic realignment on Europe, it had its uses for him, and he did not disappoint them, though he frequently let himself down.

Very early in his meteoric career, Brown had marked himself out as the man of a European future, while committed to retaining the UK nuclear deterrent. In March 1957, he said in a Labour Party political broadcast: 'I want to see this country as the leader of western Europe. I want us to have our own foreign policy, and that means the power to carry it out. I hope it is not a question of a situation in which we use the hydrogen bomb, but I can well imagine a situation where we want to use it as a threat.'

His blunt speaking, together with a suspicion that he was positioning himself for the party leadership, infuriated left-wing MPs, but marked him out as a man with whom the real powers in the country could do business. He had already made his mark in politics long before. Born in 1914, a poor boy from south London, he became a fur salesman on leaving school. He soon found he was a natural spokesman for working people and quickly moved into the labour movement as a full-time official for the Transport and General Workers' Union. The T & G was a powerhouse within the Labour Party and though he was once derided by its greatest figure, Ernie Bevin, as 'a whippersnapper', Brown was sponsored by the union in the 1945 election, entering the Commons for the Derbyshire constituency of Belper at the same time as his future rival Harold Wilson.

Thereafter his rise was rapid. Immediately appointed to the junior ranks of government as a Parliamentary Private Secretary, first to George Isaacs, Minister of Labour, and then to Chancellor Hugh Dalton in 1947, he became a minister in 1947 as Under-Secretary for Agriculture, though his urban origins in the Peabody buildings of Southwark were a far cry from the country's sodden fields. He was appointed Minister of Works in 1951 and seemed destined for high office, until Clem Attlee was driven from Downing Street by an even older Winston Churchill that year.

Brown took defeat in his stride. His naturally pugnacious temperament fitted him well for the combative politics of opposition, and by 1955 he was a member of Hugh Gaitksell's

shadow Cabinet, elected by members of the Parliamentary
Labour Party who then had sole responsibility for choosing
the leader. He was frontbench spokesman first for his old beat
of Agriculture and then Labour, before being given the hugely
important portfolio of Defence. At the height of the Cold
War, the politician most enamoured with The Bomb, which
his party was not, was responsible for fashioning a strategy to
deal with the Soviet Union. Brown went at the task in his cus-
tomary bull-at-a-gate style. In 1956, the year of the Hungarian
Revolution, he famously picked a fight with Soviet leader
Nikita Krushchev at a welcome dinner thrown by Labour's
national executive in the Harcourt Room at Westminster.
When Krushchev suggested that the Western powers had let
down the Russian war effort, Brown exploded. 'May God forgive you!' he told the old atheist Communist ruler. And when
his guest demurred, Brown piled Pelion upon Ossa, accusing
the USSR of being responsible for the deaths of brave Poles
and 'a lot of my comrades' by signing the Ribbentrop Pact.

Pandemonium ensued and Gaitskell tried to pour oil over
troubled waters with a conciliatory speech. The Russians were
both angry and bemused. Nothing like this ever happened in
Moscow, and the incident troubled them sufficiently to offer
the shadow Defence Secretary a trip to the USSR. Meanwhile,
Brown's ratings in the media and the nation shot up. Standing
up to the Russian Bear – as his excitable conduct was characterised – was immensely popular. He became a household
name, and not just in his own home where his long-suffering
wife once observed: 'He talks to them like he talks to me.'

In the sometimes stormy times that followed, Brown
affirmed in private to Gaitskell that 'I'm no man's stooge.'
He demonstrated his nerve and ambition in 1960, sens-
ing an opportunity for advancement when Wilson unwisely

challenged Gaitskell for the leadership. Brown ran for the vacant deputy leadership, beating his moderate rival James Callaghan. The role is more ceremonial than commanding, but his success confirmed his long-term aspiration to lead his party.

The ultimate prize became available with tragic swiftness, when Gaitskell died suddenly in January 1963 after a short and mysterious illness. 'I pray for his soul,' said the Christian Socialist Brown in a television tribute. 'I mourn his passing in every way.' But he confided to a previous deputy leader, Herbert Morrison, that the opportunity had 'come too soon. I'm not ready for it.' Nonetheless, he was now acting leader, and in his own bonhomous way was soon conducting a leadership campaign in the bars and lobbies of Westminster. Labour MPs were apprehensive about George's drinking and his reputation as a loose cannon. They were even more suspicious of the wily Wilson, who was all things to all men, particularly to the influential left of the PLP.

Brown gathered around him a group of like-minded MPs, including a clutch of former ministers and rising backbench stars like Roy Mason from the – then large – group of NUM-sponsored members, and with his T & G background, Brown quietly began mopping up the trade union vote. His trenchant support for the Common Market (as the EU was then usually known) and unequivocal backing for Britain's nuclear deterrent dispelled some initial fears about his volatility among the party's right-wing. James Callaghan entered the field, but garnered only forty votes in the first round and most of these transferred to Brown in the second round. He emerged victorious over Wilson, but it was a close-run thing: 130 votes to 117. Newspaper reaction was mixed. 'Up George And At 'Em!' yelled the *Daily Express*, but *The Times* editorialised 'Sooner George Brown drunk than Harold Wilson sober' – a taste of the ambiguous view of Fleet Street that was to dog his leader-ship and premiership.

Nineteen sixty-three was a very good year to become leader. The Tories had been in power for more than a decade and the nation was tiring of them. A general election could not be long postponed. The Conservative Party, too, had a relatively new leader, the aristocratic Sir Alec Douglas-Home, who baffled rather than galvanised voters. Famously unable to do his economic calculations without a supply of matchsticks, the former Earl of Home, who gave up his peerage to lead the Tories, was no match on the stump for the colourful Brown. George, who could wow a thousand-strong audience, speaking for an hour or more without notes, breathed life into a moribund election campaign in October 1964. Campaigning on the theme of 'thirteen years of Tory misrule', he travelled the country on an old-fashioned barnstorming tour more reminiscent of a US presidential candidate of the 1930s than the television age. For the duration – and, as it turned out, for good – he also forswore the attractions of Ms Keeler. His eyes were on a bigger prize.

The Swinging Sixties were still scarcely a gleam in the eye of Carnaby Street fashion retailers, and Brown's Old Testament enthusiasm stirred a chord, not least among the skilled working class whose votes had been steadily deserting to Macmillan's 'Never had it so good' Conservatives. Brown was reassuring on defence, radical on Europe (which he kept under rein) and strong on the need for jobs, by government intervention if necessary. Nevertheless, the outcome was almost a re-run of his leadership contest: Labour squeaked in by 317 seats to the Tories' 303, which, with the Speaker, the Liberals and one other, gave him an overall Commons majority of only five.

With the iron discipline he expected from his Chief Whip, Bob Mellish, it would be just enough.

Brown entered Downing Street with a characteristic flourish, in a grand, black, open-top limousine with wife Sophie by his side. 'This is an historic day for our country,' he said on the steps of No. 10, 'the first day that a working-class boy from Peabody Buildings has entered this sanctum as your Prime Minister. I intend to fulfil the faith you have placed in me, and, with God's grace, govern for all the country. Thank you.'

With that he turned through the famous black door and ordered a stiff gin and tonic. A monumental in-tray of trouble awaited him. General de Gaulle had earlier vetoed UK membership of the Common Market. His old sparring partner, Krushchev, had been ousted from the Kremlin the day Brown became Premier. In southern Rhodesia (Zimbabwe) the white minority government was threatening unilateral independence. At home, an economic crisis was pending. Britain had a balance of payments deficit approaching a billion pounds. Within weeks of assuming office, Brown was forced to go to the Commons with an emergency package of measures, hoisting income tax, fuel taxes and introducing a Capital Gains Tax, to the fury of the City.

Prime Minister Brown took a leaf out of the American book (he had an admiration bordering idolatry for President Jack Kennedy) and made a heart-to-heart appeal to the people on all TV channels. 'I have to tell you,' he declared with unusual high seriousness, 'that our country is faced with a very grave situation. The Conservative government left us with a balance of payments crisis, which international speculators are exploiting. Our currency, the pound, is under heavy pressure in the money markets, but we intend to press ahead with our programme for government. None of this is the fault of working people, but we will all have to make some sacrifices to pull the nation through. I ask for your understanding and support in the nation's hour of need.'

Brown spoke dramatically of pressing ahead, but he quietly shelved his long-cherished plans for a Department of Economic Affairs to displace the 'dead hand' of the Treasury, where he had sent Harold Wilson as a cruel and unusual punishment for seeking to thwart his ambition. Peter Shore had been appointed Paymaster-General, as a kind of Secretary of State in Waiting for a DEA, but the sheer scale of the economic crisis inherited from the Tories made it impossible to proceed with high-flown notions of centralised state planning. It was, in any event, not very much in keeping with Brown's view of the world, and had probably been cooked up as a means of upstaging Wilson's economic thinking. A DEA unit was set up inside the Treasury, with pipe-smoking ex-miner Roy Mason as its junior ministerial head, but this was merely a sop to backbenchers seeking some red socialist meat in the gruesome aftermath of the election.

If he had hoped that his October measures would quash market speculation, events proved Prime Minister Brown wrong. The nation's foreign currency reserves were depleting at a terrifying speed, falling to little more than £1 billion. A month later, interest rates were raised again, and the government was forced to go to the central bankers who guaranteed a $3 billion loan to save sterling. In his cups with close friends like Sports Minister Denis Howell (later famous as the ministerial rain-maker), George railed against the injustice of it all. 'How can they do this to me,' he would wail. 'Do you think it's class hatred? What can I do? Yes, thank you, I will have another.'

Happily, a truly momentous break lay just over the horizon,

where it truly mattered: Europe. Brown's relations with de Gaulle were more amiable than might have been supposed. The French President accepted that George's European credentials were genuine, whereas Wilson was merely opportunist on the issue. Having issued his infamous 'Non!' in 1963, he began to warm to the patriotic old rogue in No. 10. Feelers about reviving the UK's application for entry to the EEC, conducted at embassy level over several months in early 1966, resulted in ministerial exchanges in Paris and London. This was serious. Brown risked the wrath of his backbenchers and almost half his Cabinet if he went ahead with a bid to join the Common Market.

But he had an ally in unexpected quarters. By now, the Conservative Party had a new leader at the helm (sometimes quite literally). Edward Heath, another, if not quite working class, of the artisan class. He was a passionate supporter of British entry and, even though he had many doubters in his own ranks, he could deliver sufficient votes at Westminster to make the project feasible. Brown calculated that the prize would be worth the risk. 'I can do this y'know,' he confided to his Foreign Secretary, Denis Healey, newly installed after James Callaghan had been moved to the Home Office, 'I'm the only man who can.'

The calculation ran as follows: negotiations on terms for entry, if successful, could be followed up by enabling legislation to be put to the Commons. With the support of Tory MPs and the nine Liberals, Brown could get this on to the statute book, and then go to the country on a 'Europe – Our Nation's Future' ticket. It would be an enormous gamble, but if it paid off it would place him in the front rank of Britain's Premiers. He would be assured of a place in history as 'the man who got us into Europe'. The campaign would be deeply divisive, not least because opinion polls showed only a third of Britons supported entry. The trade unions were hostile. Washington was persuaded, but President Johnson was almost totally pre-occupied with the war in Vietnam and Europe felt like a side-show. Employers' organisations like the CBI and Engineering Federation could be relied on for their backing, and big (if discreet) money could be found for a 'Yes' campaign.

Wilson was furious, and intrigued for a leadership con-test. But MPs, tired of being dragooned into the voting lob-bies night after night by Mellish's thugs, saw the prospect of a Labour government with a healthy working majority. Most of them had no strong views about Europe either way, and some knew practically nothing about it. But if the proposition offered political security for five years, it was worth a punt. So they went along with the idea, without much enthusiasm but equally without subversive intent. Heath held secret talks with Brown at a Foreign Office-owned country retreat in the Sussex countryside outside Shoreham, and assured him of Conservative backing in the Commons. When news of the meeting leaked out – as these things invariably do – George faced a storm of protest, chiefly from his own side, at Westminster.

At a meeting of the PLP, Brown turned in a tour de force that silenced the rebels. 'What is your alternative?' he bel-lowed. 'You have none. So don't come here and destroy the very best opportunity this country has to secure its social, economic and political future. Where is your patriotism now? In hock to those whose loyalties lie elsewhere, or with your Prime Minister and his senior colleagues who have set us upon this course of action?' His words, particularly the reference to 'loyalties elsewhere', widely taken to mean Communist sympathies, infuriated the Labour left but delighted Fleet Street. *The Times*, uneasy about the issue, still congratulated him on a brave stand, while even the anti-EEC *Daily Express* conceded that 'here is a man who sticks up for Britain'. *The Guardian* was beside itself with excitement, hailing Brown as 'a visionary'.

With such momentum behind him, how could he not seize the day? Brown called a snap general election in late July 1966. Coincidentally, but beneficially, England won the World Cup during the campaign, beating Germany 4–2. Amid national euphoria, George took this as a good omen. Germany had kept a diplomatic silence during his political brokerage with de Gaulle, and was now thought not be a bar to UK entry. On the whole, the 'Europe – Our Future' election passed off remarkably quietly. Most people were more concerned about rising prices and increasing unemployment, but they were inclined to give 'Our George' – his TV performances were becoming more professional and more avuncular – the benefit of the doubt. Besides, the Tories had nothing fresh to offer. Brown returned to Downing Street with a stonking majority of ninety-seven, and a mandate to pursue his European dream.

George was in a hurry. In Paris, Charles was not. Having given an amber light to the negotiations, he now began to erect barricades, an intrinsic habit of the French. De Gaulle wanted specific undertakings from the British government acknowledging the diarchy of France and Germany in Europe. The UK, which he always contended was 'not a continental power', would be a second-class player in an enlarged Europe. He also demanded financial contributions that British diplomats insisted were wildly in excess of the nation's proper dues, and probably intended to make up a mounting deficit in farm subsidies. Fishing was a further stumbling block, with France insisting upon a complete right for its Channel port fishermen to trawl anywhere off the coast of the UK. And most ominously of all, de Gaulle required London to sign up to the political ideology of 'ever closer union' laid down in the Treaty of Rome.

The Foreign Office, steeped in an imperial tradition of getting its way over 'bloody foreigners', was briefly at a loss and feared a calamitous breakdown. Some unusually diplomatic footwork from Denis Healey kept the negotiations on track, and they continued right through 1967 until Brown's second major economic crisis in late autumn that year. Once more, international speculation against the pound drove sterling down to new levels, and Chancellor Roy Jenkins was obliged to accept massive support from the IMF to avert devaluation of the pound. 'That will never, never, happen in my time as Prime Minister,' Brown told the nation in his pre-Christmas TV interview. But the price was high: full support for the USA in the burgeoning war in Vietnam, including the despatch of an elite force of SAS troops to work alongside American special forces operating in the jungle against Ho Chi Minh's forces. Having fought Communism in the Transport and General Workers' Union, Brown saw no difference in principle to fighting it in south-east Asia. Few of his backbenchers agreed, and again he had to rely on Tory votes in the Commons to approve the IMF loan and its disagreeable terms.

By 1968, Brown had been leader for five years and Prime Minister for four. The strain was showing more and more. His drinking grew increasingly erratic – there were times when a single large gin would trigger an explosive outburst – and staff at No. 10 feared a public meltdown. This was before the days when 'spin doctors' choreographed their masters' every move, and though the Westminster lobby could be relied on not to report his wilder moments, the same could not be true of press photographers. The famous pictures of Brown being helped from the gutter after an interesting evening at the Irish Embassy unquestionably diminished his standing at home and abroad. No longer could his exotic behaviour be written off as 'just our lovable old George'.

He ploughed on with his life's ambition, however, and by a second great stroke of good fortune de Gaulle ran into serious domestic difficulties. He had put down the 1968 student revolution with the aid of his violent *flics*, but now in his late seventies and in failing health he had lost his ruling touch. French voters rejected his proposed reforms of the Senate and local government, and he retired in a huff once again to Colombey-les-deux-Églises. Georges Pompidou, who succeeded to the Elysee Palace, was more amenable to British entry into the EEC. Three years earlier, on a visit to London, he had urged the British government to devalue and deflate the economy to get into Europe.

With devaluation out of the way, and the British economy showing signs of revival, Brown seized the opportunity of Pompidou's accession to the presidency to inject fresh momentum into the entry talks. The French still bargained hard, but the departure of de Gaulle had removed the greatest single stumbling block. During private talks on the fringe of Pompidou's 'coronation', Brown agreed terms for UK admission that economists were later to condemn as 'crucifying'. In his haste to secure his place in history as 'the man who got us in', he saddled his countrymen with a contributions regime that beggared the nation.

But there was no stopping the bull of Belper. In the autumn of 1969, despite losing a vote on entry at the Labour Party conference in Blackpool, he presented the European Community [British Accession] Bill to the Commons. Three Cabinet members (Peter Shore, Barbara Castle and Tony Benn) resigned, and Benn went on to use his success in the Private Members'

Bill lottery to demand a nationwide referendum on both the principle and terms entry.

This 'foreign' initiative was unpopular even with anti-Europe Labour MPs, and was easily throttled at birth. Again, however, he turned to Edward Heath for support, and it was enthusiastically forthcoming from the Tory leader, if not from all his MPs. After a stormy passage, during which proceedings in the Chamber had to be suspended when maverick left-winger Konni Zilliacus seized the mace and whirled it round his head, the Bill passed by 429 votes to 171. Outside the House, pro- and anti-Europe demonstrators clashed, and police made over a hundred arrests.

But the decision was made. After Brown's private deal with Pompidou had been hammered into a formal treaty, the government won an easy Commons victory for the empowering Bill and the date for British accession was set for 1 January 1971. There could be no going back. The UK was committed, though nobody knew what the political fallout would look like. By this stage, four years after winning a landslide majority, Labour ought to have been sitting quite comfortably in the polls. The Tories had been virtually sidelined by Heath's unstinting support for the Europe Project, which prompted droves of faithful Conservatives to tear up their membership cards. The Liberals were caught in a similar bind, and it was the parties of the fringe – right-wing and nationalist – that benefited from a shift in the public mood.

This had been caused by the 1969 so-called 'winter of discontent' that broke out over Brown's imposition of a statutory prices and incomes policy, which bore down harder on people's pay than prices. Strikes, particularly in the public sector, had damaged confidence in Labour's ability to govern, and Barbara Castle's remedy, a tough new code of industrial relations embodied in her *In Place of Strife* White Paper, collapsed when she resigned from the Cabinet over Europe. The resulting vacuum was filled by a meaningless pledge of good behaviour from the TUC, but the public were not fooled.

So when an exhausted – rather than 'tired and emotional' – Brown called his second snap election in June 1970, Labour was only four points ahead in the polls. He was confident (he was rarely anything else) that the British people would reward him for the greatest single act of statesmanship since World War Two: the tying of our future to that of a booming Europe. In the long, hot early summer, he did what he knew best, stumping the country on a three-week tour that I covered as a young reporter for *The Times*.

He was met everywhere by cheering crowds, though many had been bussed in by regional party officials. He excelled as ever on the soapbox, a diminutive man with a strong, clear voice and a message in which be believed. Even his devoted enemy Richard Crossman conceded that 'George has this extraordinary public appeal, which time after time earns him public forgiveness for gross misbehaviours and deficiencies which would have been found intolerable in anybody else.' It made no difference whether it was a church hall in Great Yarmouth or a massive auditorium in Manchester, the great charmer wowed his audiences wherever he went.

And yet his poll lead slipped, slowly at first but by election day the parties were neck and neck. Heath had distinguished himself from Labour by pummelling the government over strikes and wages. He promised voters an end to statutory curbs on wages, coupled with an Industrial Relations Bill that would bring union bosses to heel. It was an attractive package to an electorate wearied of walkouts and fed on a subtle media diet of headlines like 'Now They Won't Let Us Bury Our Dead!'

On 18 June, Brown returned to Belper for the count, having spent only four days in his constituency. His seat had undergone dramatic demographic change since his first victory there in 1945, and his majority had been whittled down from 9,000 to little over 4,000. More than ten thousand new voters had joined the electoral roll, many living on new private housing estates and commuting to Derby rather than working in local industry. It was a more middle-class constituency, and Heath's 'modern' economic message reverberated more convincingly than Brown's old-fashioned Christian Socialism.

When the result was declared just before 1 a.m., it was catastrophic, not just for Brown but for his party and his government. He had been defeated by an unknown public relations man from London with a double-barrelled name, Geoffrey Stewart-Smith. It was the first time in living memory that a sitting Prime Minister had lost his seat in a general election. Brown, leaning on Sophie's arm, was clearly devastated. White-faced, he made a brief speech of thanks and returned to Downing Street by car, where he conceded defeat to Edward Heath at 3 a.m.

It was the end of his dream. His peerage was assured, and there would be many opportunities in business, in the media and a chance finally to write his memoirs, *In My Way*, a nod to the self-indulgent Frank Sinatra song which summed up all that was worst in his character. But he had desperately wanted to see the Europe Project through to reality. How he would have enjoyed sitting at the top table with the rest of Europe's leaders! The team photos, the TV press conferences, the grandstanding in the great capital cities! It had all been torn from him by the ungrateful wretches of a small Derbyshire town.

Despite still being a public figure, Lord George Brown (a nice demotic tough) went downhill after his humiliation. He quit the Labour Party in disgust at Harold Wilson's succession and its subsequent (slight) move to the left, and joined the SDP. He also abandoned his long-suffering Sophie one Christmas Eve and went to live with his mistress, Margaret Haines, a Foreign Office secretary little more than half his age. They set up house in rural Cornwall, where Brown died, half-forgotten, in 1985. The best, however, lives on. His rambunctious personality, great charm and quick mind left behind many anecdotes about George, the man. But it will be as St George, the battling politician who took us into Europe, that he will be remembered.

Prime Minister Tebbit
walks away from Maastricht

Peter Cuthbertson

It is unlikely the Tebbit years could have happened without the intervention of Frank Field, the Labour MP whose
curious relationship with Margaret Thatcher gave him real
influence, and Charles Powell, her foreign policy adviser. As
Thatcher approached the close of her tenth year as Prime
Minister, both advised her independently to stand down.
With an overheating economy and three spectacular election
victories, she would end on an unprecedented high note.
Most of all, by leaving now, she had the best chance of ensuring her favoured successor.

Thatcher's choice was her popular lieutenant Norman
Tebbit. A critic of Edward Heath before Thatcher, Tebbit
made a name for himself in her government. A former union
official himself, he had already played a key role in trade union
reform, was outspoken against sympathising with rioters
and had helped deliver a landslide election victory in 1987.
Thatcher also saw in Tebbit a reflection of her own talent for
connecting unmistakeably right-wing policies to the aspirations of working-class and lower middle-class floating voters
who decided elections.

Tebbit himself, however, was reluctant. Much later,
Thatcher admitted that from January to April 1989, affairs of

state sometimes came second for her. Her first priority was persuading Tebbit to stand for the Conservative leadership. It was only on 11 April that he committed himself unambiguously to this course, and promised to be ready when Thatcher resigned. The following month, one week after celebrating her tenth anniversary as Prime Minister, she announced her departure.

Tebbit attributed his success in the 1989 leadership contest 'as much as any other factor' to a brilliant campaign team. From the Cabinet, Nicholas Ridley, Kenneth Baker, John Major and of course the Prime Minister herself wooed most leading frontbenchers. Backbenchers were pursued by Alan Clark, Michael Portillo, Ian Gow, David Davis and John Redwood, with Chris Patten in particular managing to win over a considerable number of the backbenchers on the left of the party. The backing of the Tory press – most fiercely of all from *The Sun* – was another shot in the arm for Tebbit.

But Tebbit could have lost, had either of his opponents made way for the other. The charismatic Michael Heseltine and the weighty Geoffrey Howe both had appeal – but to almost exactly the same section of MPs.

Howe had been a great reforming Chancellor and a largely successful Foreign Secretary. But he lacked a power base within the party, and in setting forth an economic policy based around entry into the European Exchange Rate Mechanism, he endeared himself only to Heseltine's potential supporters. Nigel Lawson, the ardently pro-ERM Chancellor who ran Howe's campaign, acknowledged later that his team spent at least three times as much effort pursuing votes from MPs on the pro-European left of the party as on the right of the party, with which both men had once been identified.

For all other MPs, Tebbit had two overriding advantages: he was the only candidate for Conservatives sceptical of the ERM, and he had the unambiguous endorsement of the woman who had won the previous three general elections. Surprisingly, it was also Tebbit rather than Heseltine or Howe who dropped the strongest hints to worried MPs about ending the unpopular Community Charge (also known as the poll tax). Chris Patten, who had received private assurances, was firmer on this point and helped ensure that Tebbit won more support from the left of the party than was won from the right by Howe and Heseltine combined.

In the first (and only) ballot on 25 May, Tebbit won the narrowest of absolute majorities, with 188 votes to Heseltine's 141 and Howe's 46. But the verdict of the Parliamentary Party was clear. Thatcher's strategy had worked.

In putting together his Cabinet, Tebbit reluctantly decided that the same individuals should be kept in the three great offices of state – so long as they acknowledged the verdict of the leadership election. But Nigel Lawson and Geoffrey Howe both declined to serve under a Prime Minister who had just been elected in opposition to the Exchange Rate Mechanism, and who made clear that under him the pound also would no longer be shadowing the value of the Deutschmark. Howe in particular explained that he viewed the ERM, and eventual entry into a single European currency, as essential to Britain's economic and foreign policy.

And so a slightly relieved Tebbit decided that the key economic portfolios would be reserved for those who shared his opposition to the ERM. Nicholas Ridley, previously Environment Secretary, was made Chancellor. John Redwood was appointed to the Cabinet as Chief Secretary to the Treasury.

But Tebbit was determined to incorporate all wings of the Conservative Party in the Cabinet. Douglas Hurd, the Home Secretary, was appointed as the new Foreign Secretary and replaced at the Home Office by Kenneth Clarke. Michael Heseltine accepted the role of Environment Secretary, and set about dismantling the Community Charge.

John Major and Chris Patten were rewarded generously, with Tebbit recognising that both had supported him when they could as easily, or more easily, have backed either of his opponents. Major became Defence Secretary and Patten the leader of the House of Commons. Media commentators rightly interpreted the appointment of Alan Clark as Northern Ireland Secretary, with Ian Gow as Minister of State, as signifying a particularly robust approach towards the Irish Republican Army – the IRA bombing in Brighton five years previously had left Tebbit's wife in a wheelchair.

The economy was the greatest initial challenge for the new government. Nicholas Ridley's predecessor, in an effort to prevent the pound rising against the Deutschmark, had been increasing the money supply substantially. The resultant inflation had reached 8.3 per cent by June 1989, and interest rates had already risen to 14 per cent in an effort to slow down the economy.

The end of the policy of shadowing the Deutschmark halted any further rise in inflation. Interest rates remained high for the next twelve months and economic growth was choked. The economy briefly dipped into a quickly forgotten recession in 1990, but by the time Tebbit celebrated his first year in Downing Street, inflation was back to the levels of the mid-1980s and interest rates were permitted to fall.

Sterling's value against the Deutschmark fell with each cut in interest rates. This angered some, but the Chancellor pointed to Bank of England projections that interest rates would have to rise back to at least 14 per cent if Britain entered the ERM. Such a policy, Ridley argued, would surely mean a deep recession – and even then would risk the financial markets one day ignominiously ejecting sterling from the ERM.

Instead, the economy began the period of strong economic growth and annual tax cuts that characterised the Tebbit years. This economic recovery began within months of the end of Gulf War, in which Iraq was ejected from Kuwait successfully with very light British casualties.

It fell to Tebbit's two successors to secure peace in Northern Ireland, but military historians agree that the early 1990s were most significant in beginning the long peace process. After Tebbit became Prime Minister, the death toll on the Republican side began to rise, and no major bombs were exploded on the British mainland until the following year.

It was on a rainy Monday – 8 January 1990 – that the Army Council of the IRA met in a private home on a quiet street in Dundalk, just south of the Irish Republic's border with Ulster. This council included Gerry Adams and Martin McGuinness, the two most prominent Sinn Fein leaders of the era, and five leading IRA paramilitaries. Neighbours gave the only eyewitness accounts, in which the sound of sub-machine gun fire began at around 8.20 p.m. and less than ten minutes later at least a dozen men, all in black, disappeared in the direction of a nearby field. Adams, one of the world's best-known terrorist leaders of the 1980s, had been shot eighteen times. The only surviving member of the IRA Army Council was Freddie Scappaticci, whose survival was unexplained at the time, but who was eventually unmasked as a British agent.

The Prime Minister gave a statement detailing the many killings for which the IRA's Army Council had been responsible and welcoming the 'opportunity for peace that may now follow its surprising demise'. The Labour leader, Neil Kinnock, issued no immediate statement, but was forced to act when one of his frontbenchers, Harriet Harman, argued that this 'atrocity' had made Gerry Adams a 'martyr'. Kinnock separated her from her shadow Cabinet portfolio position within hours and a hitherto promising career was ended.

Accusations of British complicity in the assassinations came from a number of quarters. The professionalism of the operation, and the fact that none of the Loyalist terror groups came forward to claim responsibility, meant that the government struggled to dismiss the accusations as the words of unhinged conspiracy theorists. When the government refused to conduct a full inquiry into the incidents of 8 January, a diplomatic incident seemed inevitable. At one point the Irish government was hours away from withdrawing its ambassador, but Tebbit and his Foreign Secretary Douglas Hurd successfully persuaded Ireland's Taoiseach Charles Haughey that this could irreparably damage any hopes of peace.

Even before the IRA reprisals of 3 March, in which bombs were exploded in London, Manchester and Glasgow, killing forty, there was no evidence from opinion polls that the government suffered electorally from accusations of complicity. After the attacks, public opinion swung even more behind the government.

Flanked by his wife Margaret, the Prime Minister gave a statement outside 10 Downing Street in which information from intelligence reports was divulged to the public in unprecedented detail. Tebbit argued that the attacks were the last gasp of a leaderless organisation paralysed by infighting over what direction to take. Voters were split on whether Tebbit had known of, or had any involvement in, the events of 8 January. But in a MORI poll a week after the March bombings, 74 per cent of the public agreed that 'Whether or not the government was involved, the assassination of the IRA leadership was a good thing'. In Parliament, there were echoes of the Falklands War eight years earlier, as Labour and Liberal Democrat front-benchers all endorsed the government's resolute stance.

The number of British troops in Ulster tripled by the end of March, and the deaths of IRA volunteers rose even faster, peaking in mid 1991. We now know that the long peace process began with a secret IRA communication to Downing Street stating simply: 'We know the war is over but we need your help to end it.' Within less than fifteen years, the IRA men who sent that message went on to be junior ministers in a devolved Northern Ireland Assembly. It would almost certainly have happened in under a decade had they accepted that the British government would not agree to give terrorists early release. Eventually, two Prime Ministers later, the IRA and other terrorist groups on both sides of the conflict dropped this demand, abandoned the 'armed struggle' and committed themselves to rancorous but almost entirely peaceful electoral politics in a new devolved administration.

Almost immediately after the November 1991 general election, which Tebbit won with a majority of seventy-four, the Conservatives faced the greatest crisis of Tebbit's premiership as the European Community pushed ahead in a far more federalist direction. The negotiations for the Treaty of Maastricht began just one month after Tebbit's election success. The Treaty meant a single currency, a Common Foreign and Security Policy and a Social Charter aimed at curbing the ability of member states to deregulate their labour markets. The consensus on the continent was strongly in favour of moves towards a European Union. Within the government, arguments raged fiercely. The Foreign Secretary, supported by the Environment Secretary Michael Heseltine, urged that while the government should aim to influence its content, Britain must sign whatever

Treaty emerged. The Prime Minister and Chancellor argued that Britain could retain the benefits of EC membership without taking any further steps towards federalism.

Speaking in the House of Lords in January 1992, Lady Thatcher declared her opposition to any government that signed a Maastricht Treaty along the lines detailed the previous month. At Prime Minister's Questions the same day, Tebbit was challenged by the Labour leader John Smith to disassociate himself from Thatcher's comments. Instead the Prime Minister endorsed them.

Douglas Hurd and Michael Heseltine resigned from the government the same day. They and fourteen other Tory backbenchers – instantly dubbed the 'Maastricht rebels' – began their campaign for the Treaty of Maastricht. Labour and Liberal Democrats MPs were almost unanimous in support. But Tebbit, having just won the Conservatives a fourth general election with a big working majority, retained the confidence of his party and the House of Commons. Despite the passionate efforts of the Maastricht rebels, the Treaty never went before the floor of the House of Commons. The European Community began its steps towards federalism without the continent's best performing economy. Within a decade, nearly all of the other members shared a currency and a central bank. In return for Britain's acquiescence to the emergence of a quasi-federal Europe, the other member states agreed to Britain beginning moves towards bilateral free trade agreements with North America, South America and large parts of Asia.

In the reshuffle triggered by the resignations of Hurd and Heseltine, the Chancellor chose to leave the government. Claims of ill health were viewed sceptically – a scepticism which ended only with Ridley's death from lung cancer the following year. The pro-European Home Secretary, Kenneth

Clarke, had been tempted to resign with Hurd and Heseltine but this was quickly forgotten with the offer of the Treasury. The Employment Secretary Michael Howard was appointed to replace Clarke at the Home Office. John Major, a popular Defence Secretary during the Gulf War, became Foreign Secretary. The reshuffle was also notable for the appointment of Nirj Deva to a junior role within the Department of Trade and Industry. The newly elected MP became Britain's first Asian minister of modern times. Three years later he was the first Asian Cabinet Minister.

John Redwood was appointed Education Secretary. Redwood immediately began work on two of the most radical changes of the Tebbit years. Free university degrees were abolished for those without full scholarships from the institutions themselves. Fees for tuition, introduced initially at very low levels and to be repaid over two decades, were opposed bitterly by many students, but the public was largely indifferent. Many academics were secretly delighted at this new source of funding – and later open defenders of higher fees.

Labour and Liberal Democrat spokesmen were adamant that forcing students to incur debt to pay for their education would make a university degree the preserve of wealthier middle-class families. But while there is no evidence of a fall in the number of dim young people from wealthy families who went to university, there was a dramatic rise in state school admissions to top universities from the mid-1990s onwards. Redwood attributed this to what the journalist Michael Gove – himself an outspoken supporter – was to nickname the 'free schools' policy.

After Redwood, any individual, group or organisation wishing to establish a school could receive state funding in proportion to the number of pupils educated there. Overwhelmingly, it was private sector companies that entered the market and competition was fierce. But this only put parents of school-age children in control. Sceptical at first, people soon appreciated choice in education as keenly as they had accepted the withdrawal of state control from the great utilities of the 1980s. While most voters had no school-aged children, the millions who did treasured the control that school choice gave them. Polling from the period suggests that opposition to school choice was one of Labour's greatest electoral problems in the 1990s – highlighted continually when the party sided with the teaching unions in outrage every time a failing state school closed because of competition from the third sector. The issue split Labour down the middle in the 1990s, aiding the electoral prospects of a Conservative Party that had already been in office for more than fifteen years.

In a candid passage in his memoirs, Tebbit described the absence of welfare reform as his government's greatest failing. He deemed his victory in cutting crime to be its greatest achievement.

Prior to Tebbit and Howard, the conventional wisdom on crime was deep-rooted and cross-party. Evidence-based policies that accounted for the failure of community punishments to protect the public were taboo. If prisoners reoffended after release, it was taken as proof that prison should be used less rather than more. Michael Howard's determined increase in the prison population ended this culture – and appears to have been integral to the great crime decline of the 1990s. Today's cross-party consensus in support of prison is a remarkable reversal from the opposite consensus, which prevailed from the 1960s until the 1990s. Few historians now dispute that overturning this consensus was central to Britain's transition from a high-crime to a low-crime society.

Feverish speculation about a general election in 1995 proved unfounded. Instead, the Prime Minister let it slip in a television interview in December of that year that he intended to retire from the House of Commons at the next election to look after his wife full time. Whether he intended to trigger an immediate leadership contest or not, that was the outcome, and Tebbit put up little struggle when he was pressured to make way quickly to allow a successor to prepare for a general election in 1996. As it turned out, Tebbit spent the former half of 1996 as a backbench Member of Parliament, keenly defending his record from Labour attacks.

As with his predecessor, Tebbit retired popular in Britain, disliked in Brussels and respected globally. Like her, he managed both to enrage Britain's establishment and to force it to accommodate his politics. As with Thatcher, the effects of his years in Downing Street are difficult to overestimate, and can be expected to continue inspiring controversy for generations.

Prime Minister Foot saves the economy and the Labour government

Anne Perkins

Almost the only people who guessed Harold Wilson would shortly retire were the drivers in the government car pool. It was they, naturally interested in future jobs, who observed that he had changed the rules about cars and drivers for former Prime Ministers. On the face of it the change simply meant that the ex-Conservative party leader and Prime Minister Ted Heath, who had just been unseated by Margaret Thatcher, had a car for life. But so too, the drivers quickly spotted, would Wilson.

For almost all of his Cabinet colleagues, the news came from nowhere. Far from seeming ready to go, Wilson had been paranoid about attempts to replace him for years, spotting plots – of which there were several – even where there were none. And then, Tuesday 16 March 1976 was an extraordinary moment to choose to retire. It was true that he had just celebrated his sixtieth birthday; it had been a muted celebration, however. The economy, in crisis throughout the 1970s, had just been through another trough. Unemployment was above the one million mark and climbing remorselessly. Prices were rising at more than 20 per cent a year; pay, even faster. Only five days before Wilson's announcement, Denis Healey, the robust and combative Chancellor, had introduced more spending cuts, picking a spectacular fight in the Commons which culminated in a serious revolt from the left and defeat in the final vote. A confidence motion had been won by a margin of seventeen.

At the same time, a breathtakingly audacious legislative programme was underway. It included curbing private medicine, trying to encourage investment in industry while also nationalising the shipbuilding and aerospace industries, and introducing devolution for Scotland and Wales. Already there had been far-reaching employment and trade union rights legislation, and a referendum in which the pro-European right of the party had been allowed to campaign against the party line, contributing to a massive victory for the 'Yes' campaign. It had, some observers warned, laid the foundations for the final split in the party.

On the morning of 16 March, Wilson – having satisfied his ambition to win a record number of elections as Labour leader as well as become the longest serving Prime Minister on record – had been to the Palace before he met his ministers. There was to be no retreat by this most notoriously fickle of politicians. The press even had the letter of resignation that the Cabinet now read for the first time. Well before the thunderstruck ministers trooped out to face the cameras in Downing Street, the leadership contest was under way.

Only Jim Callaghan, Foreign Secretary, was not troubling himself unduly: Wilson had tipped him off at Christmas that he was planning to go, although Callaghan did not quite believe him. He was equally sceptical of Wilson's apparent wish that the older man – for so long his bitter rival – should succeed him. But that Callaghan was the anointed successor was the almost universal view. He began the contest as the clear favourite. He was the man most likely to hold the neurotic party together over the rest of the parliament, and still give it the widest appeal at the next election.

Callaghan had more admirers outside the Parliament than within it. He was a reluctant European, but he was a hawk on defence, public spending cuts and – increasingly – pay restraint. As the wily opponent of trade union reform in the 1960s, he had been dubbed 'keeper of the cloth cap' by the astute political columnist Peter Jenkins. His traditionalist style and avuncular manner were steady and calming to anxious voters. The faintly bucolic image endeared him to many outside politics as much as it incensed the radicals within.

A 'Stop Jim' movement was taking shape in his critics' minds before the Foreign Secretary had crossed the road from Downing Street to the grand apartments of the Foreign Office. It was a remote hope, and there was only one obvious candidate, a man who had made unexpected friends across the party since he had joined the government only two years earlier. Michael Foot, Employment Secretary, romantic, anti-nuclear campaigner, bibliophile, literary essayist and devoted defender of Parliament offered the best chance of bringing together the reasonable right and the reasonable left. Barbara Castle, his flatmate of forty years earlier, was pushing him to stand before they were out of the Cabinet room.

Foot himself hesitated. It was not from any calculation about winning – few of his supporters supposed that was likely, and it certainly was not in his mind – but about clipping Callaghan's wings. It would be a public demonstration of the weight of the left, a base from which to demand significant jobs and influence on policy. Encouraged by the young left – people like Neil Kinnock, the new MP for Bedwelty and a neighbour of Foot's in south Wales – and older friends like John Silkin, he was persuaded that he had an obligation to defend the platform of the left, not only against the right but against Tony Benn's more radical ideas for democratic reform that were attracting support outside Westminster. Benn, who had also decided to run, made much of his ambition not to be Prime Minister, but to be leader of the Labour Party.

Callaghan made a fatal mistake. With a heavy overseas schedule, he decided he did not need to campaign. Foot, on the other hand, who envisaged the period of the leadership only as an opportunity to make the case for the programme and the kind of politics that he wished to promote, worked hard with speeches and interviews to woo the small band of 318 fellow Labour MPs that composed the electorate. A natural campaigner, in the previous six years he had stood for the deputy leadership four times. He had been an MP – with one interruption – since 1945 and a critic on the sidelines for most of those years. But in 1970 he stood for shadow Cabinet and in 1974 he became employment secretary; he had shown himself both loyal and pragmatic in the defence of agreed policy.

Even colleagues like Roy Jenkins, with whom he disagreed on almost every important political point, remained on good terms personally. It was partly a question of charm, partly a mutual intellectual respect. They might regard one another as misguided, but the man who could work in close partnership with Enoch Powell to prevent reform of the House of Lords would have no trouble finding a way of rubbing along with someone who was at least in the same party (although some rivalries were were undeniably more bitter). After the first ballot, Foot emerged in front while Jenkins, disappointed to be a distant third, dropped out along with Tony Crosland and Tony Benn. In the second round, Benn's votes and some of Crosland's went to Foot but Callaghan came out narrowly ahead, with Healey trailing on thirty-eight.

At that point a Callaghan victory seemed inescapable. And it was not Michael Foot who interrupted his smooth upward ascent – it was Denis Healey. Healey, brilliant, independent-minded and widely experienced, was a figure of the right but he had never been one of the clique around either Jenkins or Tony Crosland. He operated alone. But as Chancellor for the past two years, he was deeply troubled by the state of the economy. He knew worse would come before there was even a chance of better news. Believing a Foot victory would be the final blow to the beleaguered pound and the fragile sterling reserves, he chose to renew the battle with the left, which had been joined earlier that month in the debate over public spending.

He hoped that his intervention, in an interview with *The Guardian* published on the morning of the vote, would deliver his thirty-eight supporters to Callaghan and guarantee his victory. Instead, his remarks were widely taken as a warning that a victory for a candidate of the right would be a licence to try to silence the left in perpetuity. Healey took the attack beyond the persistent reluctance of left-wing MPs to acknowledge that public spending had to be restrained at some points, to what was happening to the party beyond Westminster and the increasingly lunatic (his word) policies being foisted on the government.

In a broad sweep of invective, he derided Michael Foot's 'moral cowardice' in front of the unions and deplored the partnership between the employment secretary and the leader of the transport workers union, Jack Jones, that had delivered industrial peace but at the apparent expense of untrammelled union power. He deplored the rate at which wages had been allowed to rise, driving up inflation and damaging profitability and the potential for investment. Not that he attacked only Labour colleagues. He also ridiculed, as only Healey could, the pusillanimous management that allowed itself to be railroaded by its employees.

The result, in terms of the numbers involved, was small. Perhaps twenty-five MPs changed their votes. The consequences were huge. On 5 April, an ashen-faced Michael Foot was ushered into the grand committee room of the House of Commons to be anointed the new leader in front of his colleagues who were as astonished as he. Within minutes, the Queen's private secretary Sir Martin Charteris was on the phone, inquiring when (but not if) it would be convenient for her first republican Prime Minister to come to the Palace to kiss hands.

Foot's republicanism was the least of the country's worries about its new leader. Foot knew what the next day's headlines were likely to say. In a moment of bleak humour in the tense hours of negotiation that followed the moment of triumph, he and his new private office competed in predicting the reaction of the press. They were not disappointed – officials at least shared the anxiety – but, as one admitted afterwards, none matched the reality of the newspapers that were delivered soon after midnight.

The Sun was black-edged, in mourning, it declared, for British democracy. The *Daily Mail* reported queues to book flights out of the country. The *Daily Express* confidently announced that the entire royal family had already made plans to take refuge in Greece, or possibly Spain. The *Telegraph* revealed that a Norfolk landowner was leaving aboard his barge, moored in readiness on the Wash, to sail across the North Sea to safety. The announcement of Foot's victory had come after the markets had closed for the day but the *Financial Times* warned of economic catastrophe, a new run on sterling and probable national bankruptcy.

Those initial 48-hours would be decisive. Foot, often so donnish and vague, recognised the need to act swiftly and as far as possible to bind up the wounds in the party while reassuring the world outside. Cabinet-making is important in any party. In Labour in the 1970s, where the balance of power between the varying factions was finely calibrated, it was high art. Foot's first and most important challenge was to persuade Denis Healey to stay in government, at the Treasury. He knew the global financial community and in turn they trusted him, if not his party. Without him – and after his onslaught it seemed all too possible – Foot's tenure of No. 10 would be short indeed.

Healey and Foot were old adversaries. They had fought over nuclear disarmament for more than twenty years, Healey irritated by what he thought of as Foot's undergraduate love of debating points, Foot frustrated by Healey's refusal to engage with his own argument. But their impatience with one another had mellowed a little in the previous two years. Healey, as he had so unmistakably shown in his *Guardian* interview, was no admirer of Foot's pacific approach to relations with the unions, but he had been impressed by his loyalty to policies he personally disagreed with and his readiness to work for the government as a whole.

As importantly, Foot was prepared to put maintaining Labour in power ahead of every other consideration. The party, in his mind, was always a coalition that had to accommodate views from the centre right to the left. He might have been an acolyte of Aneurin Bevan in the terrible days of destructive schism in the early 1950s, but he was also his biographer. He understood Bevan's rapprochement with his bitter rival Hugh Gaitskell towards the end of the decade. For Foot, politics were a matter of profound belief, and he argued for them with passion and occasional anger in the public domain. (His attack on the judge who oversaw Heath's industrial relations court was notorious, at least among Tories, for its constitutional impropriety.) Within the party, his colleagues acknowledged that he behaved with honour and courtesy.

And of course, he and Healey were both members of the Byron Society, slender ground for compromise in the wake of the intemperate attack that Foot had studied with alarm only that morning. But Healey too was both a patriot and a party loyalist. He knew that he had to stay at the Treasury if sterling was to have any chance of surviving, and he knew he had to work with Foot – as he had seen Foot working with Wilson despite their long-nurtured antipathy – if the party was not to split. At their meeting, shortly after Foot's return from the Palace, Healey was straightforward. He demanded complete control of economic policy. Foot, no economist, refused him a veto over industrial policy, one of the policy areas most keenly defended by the left, and insisted on retaining consultative rights over relations with the unions. Healey hesitated, and agreed.

As for Callaghan, he was shaken but not profoundly disappointed by defeat in a contest for a job that he had ceased to covet some years earlier. Foot assured him he could stay at the Foreign Office if he wanted to. He asked for time to consider his position. Within twenty-four hours, Callaghan confirmed that he would retire from active politics to his Sussex farm.

It was one problem solved, and it provided Foot with another opportunity to signal his determination to heal the party's wounds. He was suspicious of Roy Jenkins as a politician; he was also unable to understand why he would elevate the importance of a single policy – joining the EEC – over inflicting a potentially fatal defeat on the Conservatives by opposing it, as he had done during the passage of the European Communities Act in 1972. His own opposition to the Common Market was founded less on reservations about the damage it did to the UK economy (the position of most anti-Europeans) than on a romantic determination to defend Westminster's sovereignty against Brussels. But the matter had been settled in a referendum less than a year earlier; there was nothing to be done about it now. Putting Jenkins at the Foreign Office would largely remove him from domestic politics while indicating to the wider world a genuine openness of attitude on Foot's part. And it was, Foot had a hunch, the only job that would keep Jenkins in a Foot government. As he put it to an aide, the appeal of dining for his country, in generally agreeable company, could be the factor that kept the most influential voice on the right within the fold. In truth, if he was to keep the party together and in power, Foot's room for manoeuvre was strictly limited.

Nor was it clear that the new leader had any taste for the job that he had so unexpectedly landed. In all his long career he had demonstrated the reverse: he disliked telling people what to do and he hated restricting the liberty of others. He also had a dangerous tendency always to see the best even in the most awkward of colleagues. When his new Cabinet met for the first time less than forty-eight hours after he became Prime Minister, it was clear that his would be the style of the chairman, and a very relaxed chairman, rather than heavily engaged chief executive. His reputation as a highly informal Secretary of State (although a series of major employment Bills had issued from the department in his short time there) who had a tendency to keep the television on in his office during Test cricket was to be maintained in No. 10, although possibly without the cricket.

Foot had been as astonished as anyone at his triumph. But – keenly supported by his wife Jill Craigie's enthusiasm and determination – he began to envisage a prime ministerial role that his bibliophile-orator hero Disraeli might have recognised. He would be the party's strategist, a mediator within it, but first and foremost a campaigner in the world beyond.

There was no doubt that Labour needed a good salesman. The Tories had a sixteen-point advantage in the polls. But they also had their own problems: the new, relatively young and female leader, Margaret Thatcher, had won the party leadership in a victory even more unexpected than Foot's own. But unlike Foot, she did not have the discipline of office, nor the power of patronage, to bind the senior figures of her party to her. After little more than a year as Conservative leader, there was already talk of a coup against her. Her antagonism to the state and her approach to public spending were anathema almost as much to the policy chiefs in Conservative Central Office as they were to Labour. But Foot, always an admirer of strong women, appreciated that she was making a powerful case for arguing that Keynesianism had had its day. He took no interest in economic detail, but he could perceive that the level of unemployment, the rate of inflation and the continuing rise in public spending could not be sustained. He found himself talking not only to his old friends on the left like Neil Kinnock and Albert Booth about the dilemma, but to some of the younger MPs on the right, like Shirley Williams and Roy Hattersley. The question they debated was what to do about it. Thatcher, if not her party, wanted the state to retreat. Foot wanted to find ways to make the essentials of Keynes work. No student of contemporary economic theory, he was persuaded by proposals for a massive investment from both state and private sectors in industry and he wanted workers involved in management as a device for education and as a weapon of moderation.

Above all, Foot wanted to warn voters at large what was at stake. His greatest political strengths were his journalism and his oratory; talents that belonged more to the age of his heroes, to Disraeli and Hazlitt, than to the era of television and press releases (the latter were always a particular challenge, for he rarely read his prepared text when delivering a speech). It had been many years since there had been a prime minister so well-equipped and so ready to use his office to campaign between elections. But hints of Thatcher's planned attack on the state allowed him to reaffirm the case for democratic socialism to an audience that had not grown deaf to the importance of the collective over the individual. In speeches, articles and interviews he reiterated what was at stake, depicting what he called the 'meanness' of the Thatcher approach that would make the poorest pay for a crisis, that would allow unemployment to rise without intervention, that most dangerously would ignore the democratic will of the people and thus imperil democracy itself.

Foot's warnings, however, were issued against a backdrop of unrelentingly depressing economic news. Pay restraint – with increases restricted to £6 a week – would come to be seen as an extraordinary tool in promoting equality, one which lifted the pay of the poorest and held down the pay of almost everyone else. But it was delivered through co-operation with the trade unions, rather than by the force of law. In return, concessions were demanded in employment legislation that troubled the right, and even the old liberal conscience of Michael Foot himself. The unions wanted legal backing for the closed shop, where all workers were compelled to join a trade union. The battle was to become a turning point in relations between organised labour and the government.

Foot had had no honeymoon as Prime Minister: rather, the press had almost universally attacked him from the moment he took office. But his first six months were marked more by his series of speeches explaining what his government wanted to achieve rather than by any marked crisis. Indeed, from a very low beginning his ratings began, slowly, to improve. Voters came to appreciate the humour in his remark that no job was worth having if it involved a new suit of clothes, and to realise that his lack of interest in sartorial matters was a reflection of his deep interest in improving the well-being of his country. (He took comfort from the support the Queen Mother always offered among the raised eyebrows on state occasions). The attacks from the newspapers that had once belonged to one of his heroes, Lord Beaverbrook, never entirely faded, but they were more often found inside than on the front.

But if Foot was off the front pages, it was often because his Chancellor Denis Healey had replaced him there. Against the dollar, the pound's value declined inexorably, (from $2 just before Wilson's resignation to $1.80 in mid-May to $1.70 in June). Partly, this was the Treasury and the Bank of England operating their own devalue-deflate policy to compensate for the rise in wages and industrial costs. A devalued pound made exports cheaper and imports less so. But in attempting to improve the trade balance, they overshot. In order to stop the pound going into freefall a large loan had to be negotiated from most of the central banks of the rich world. Healey forced through another round of cuts. In September, the Bank decided it had done enough to support the pound, which immediately crashed. Meanwhile the loan of the early summer was soon due for repayment. Crisis was alarmingly imminent, and it was not a crisis that could be charmed away by high moral oratory.

The end of September is the traditional party conference season. Michael Foot was preparing his first speech as leader. Healey, having holidayed at home to look after the pound like an anxious parent keeping an eye on a teenage child, was about to fly out to Hong Kong to meet Commonwealth finance ministers – key players, for many of them kept their reserves in sterling. Then he was to go on to Manila for the annual meeting of the IMF. Should he go, he wondered. Foot was (as ever) relaxed and encouraged him to take his own decision. Healey delayed his departure by twenty-four hours, just long enough to agree with his officials that a new loan from the IMF was unavoidable. It was not the first time the country had had to sacrifice its sovereignty to the demands of the world's bankers, after all. It had been almost a regular feature throughout the 1960s and into the early 1970s. The difference this time was that Healey knew how devastating their demands were likely to be. Better to be in Manila anticipating them, he concluded, than in Blackpool confronting the irreconcilables. Healey resumed his journey to the Far East.

Blackpool 1976 was a seminal experience for Michael Foot. In the short term, he knew he could not say what some of the growing number of left-wing trade union leaders and constituency delegates wanted to hear. In this one chaotic week at the seaside, the trade union block vote committed the party to nationalisation of the insurance industry, the major clearing banks and one merchant bank. It was not a good backdrop for negotiations for a multi-billion pound loan from the IMF. In vain, Foot tried to set out an explanation, with frequent references to Aneurin Bevan, of the need to invest for the future, to hold down pay in order not to eat the seed corn that would feed future generation, to acknowledge short-term limits on what the state could spend. He was heard – if at all – in a mood of benign contempt. Yet the very mauling he received from his party rescued him in the eyes of the wider public. Against the wild-eyed Bennites, Foot increasingly sounded rational and principled.

And the national focus was on Healey's peregrinations in the Far East, where the Chancellor's confidence and negotiating skills were also beginning to show some reward. At the reassuring prospect of an IMF guarantee, pressure on the pound eased a little. Nonetheless, when the IMF arrived in London in November to discuss the terms on which they would make their loan, the atmosphere was tough. The IMF negotiators were not interested in the art of the possible: theirs was the language of the inevitability of fiscal retrenchment. For a month the argument was pursued. Foot handed Healey the sole authority in the negotiations, retaining only a veto over the final deal. Meanwhile he continued to set out a case for calm and a defence of all that Labour wanted to preserve, against a chorus of doom from the Tories.

In agreement with Healey, Foot began to broaden his discussion of Britain's economic options, even taking his case abroad, where he was little known, hoping to find the vital loan from other sources on better terms. After all, it was the UK's defence commitments – commitments Foot had questioned for as long as he had been an MP – that ate into the national finances. He began to speculate about withdrawing troops from Germany. He would like to have pondered the cost of the nuclear deterrent, but Healey and Jenkins made it clear that it could not come to that.

Yet when Healey came to him with the terms of the loan, Foot was aghast. The starting point had been a public sector borrowing requirement of £22 billion over two years. The IMF had demanded cuts in spending of £7 billion over the same period – 6 per cent in 1977–78, and 8 per cent in the next year. It would have devastated all the government's plans for industrial investment, and jeopardised commitments on pensions and health spending. This was precisely the agenda on which the Conservatives were campaigning and against which Foot had been arguing ever since becoming leader.

The first meeting between Healey and Foot was a private affair. Healey could see no alternative to the cuts. Foot, who had campaigned angrily against cuts in similar circumstances ten years earlier, was adamant that one must be found. What was most important, though, was that the meeting remained if not amiable then purposeful. Neither man was looking for an excuse to resign. Both were desperate to find a way through that would protect the Labour government and its plans for the economy. Both knew that the largesse of North Sea oil and its opportunity to restructure British industry was nearly at hand. Both interpreted the question as one of holding off the forces of massive deflation – and virtually inevitable electoral defeat that would accompany it.

Foot's travels as Prime Minister had taken him around the country, and as well as big set-piece speeches, he had been talking to party workers. Representing a south Wales constituency dominated by miners, Foot had long since lost the feel he had had in his days as a Plymouth MP for the concerns of those who were not in work, or who had no powerful union to protect them. Now he began to understand how Labour's efforts to redraw the economy seemed quite irrelevant to people who simply wanted a job and the chance to get on. He began to see that the trade unions might indeed be a necessary, but were perhaps not the only, precondition for the success of socialism. He met trade unionists who were doing well; but he also met people who told him that, as far as they were concerned, a few big unions were grabbing everything at their expense.

Foot's strength as leader was that he was always willing to listen. He deeply disliked imposing his will on others. Discontent with the power of the unions was not the only thing that he learned about on his travels. He began to perceive there was an undemocratic left at work that was intent on capturing the machinery of the party. Bitter though his memories were of the use of the party machine against the left in the 1930s and again in the 1950s, and only two years after the list of organisations considered incompatible with Labour membership had, in a spirit of tolerance, been withdrawn, he once again set NEC inquiries in process to monitor the activities of the Militant Tendency, a secretive Trotskyite grouping that was already a powerful influence in a handful of constituencies.

But the immediate significance of what he came to call his awakening was that he was forced to reconsider the short-term impact of trade union power. His own comfortable intellectual background lent a grand romance to the authenticity of a working class leader like Jack Jones, the Liverpool docker's son who fought for the Republicans in Spain. He remained committed to the role of trade unions in a socialist polity. But he began to question the impact of what Jones was seeking, ultimately, to achieve: it was not what he understood as democracy. If Europe was a threat to the sovereignty of Westminster, so too was untrammelled trade unionism.

One of the first pieces of employment legislation that Jones and Foot had agreed after 1974 had been the disbanding of the Conservatives' industrial courts and the introduction of employment and work place protection. In the short term, it was impossible to deliver everything on Jones's shopping list. Later, there would be an Act that delivered total dock workers' control of labour within Britain's coastal strip. But what caused the intuitive liberal in Foot to revolt was the demand for a closed shop. He could understand why the unions wanted it, but he was alienated by the idea of statutory limits on any worker's freedom. In particular, the closed shop in his old trade of journalism was, he knew, potentially a brake on freedom of speech.

Foot's reappraisal of the relations between government and unions was accelerated by the need to find alternatives to cuts. Trade unions had already accepted what for some was a tough pay limit in the £6 cap: for many, it meant a fall in their standard of living as inflation outstripped any pay rise. The deal was due to last until August. In July the TUC accepted that the maximum increase – although based on percentages again – should be limited to a maximum of £4 in a deal that would last for another two years. It was an extraordinary commitment from the trade unions, delivered by Jack Jones, that actually denied his members their most powerful weapon: collective bargaining.

But against the broader background of inflation, economic uncertainty and the relentless portrayal of unrestrained union might, it seemed a nugatory gain. Foot bitterly resented what seemed to him to be the unrestrained power for the press to interpret the political scene to Labour's disadvantage. But he could not avoid it. And while he would never have acted in order to appease the populist press, his instincts were against a closed shop for journalists. If he blocked it early, there would be the added bonus of heading off what was potentially a very damaging line of attack.

Foot's evangelism for the purposes of democratic socialism had not quite set the country on fire. But the climate was milder than had seemed possible only months earlier. Into this relatively benign atmosphere he lobbed the idea that there was a limit to what the law could offer trade unions by way of protection. Health and safety, occupational pensions, a state-backed arbitration process and even class actions against employers were acceptable. The closed shop was not. And at this point – although not easily, and not without a good deal of sabre rattling – the unions accepted that there was a point at which 'their' government could not promote their interests above those of other citizens. In return, Foot pledged an end to pay restraint.

None of this happened overnight. But the intent was plain. It came at the expense of the support of a handful of left-wing MPs – enough, on a bad day, to threaten the government's majority and at the end of the two-year £4 deal, there was a surge in pay settlements. But it also meant that the other major ambition of Foot's government, to devolve power to Scotland and Wales, which had a different group of opponents, had a chance of success.

The devolution of power away from Westminster was an exercise unprecedented in the twentieth century. Like Europe, it was a new politics that transcended the familiar post-war divisions of left and right. But while Europe had become the wholly-owned territory of the right, devolution had a broader appeal. Most importantly, Labour opponents were fewer and the prospects for Liberal support were clear. The Liberals had other reasons for being willing to consider an arrangement where they would support the government in return for concessions on specific policy areas: they wanted future elections to the European parliament to be conducted under some form of proportional representation. If they could also get separate Scottish and Welsh devolution Bills, while fending off an election which looked potentially disastrous for them, it would be a valuable step to more extensive constitutional reform.

Buying time, Foot too was beginning to appreciate, might not be the worst option for his premiership: time to build support for genuinely socialist objectives, and to remind the electorate what had been achieved and what might be squandered if an election was lost. He was also increasingly aware, thanks to Tony Benn, that there was always going to be an irreconcilable element on the left, and the Labour leader's job was to prevent it growing damagingly large not by satisfying its every demand but by standing up to it where necessary. He saw that even the power of trade unions could only expand in line with the acceptance of a majority of voters. Trade union membership, now approaching 11 million, was higher than it had ever been. Ever growing numbers of political levy-paying supporters were claimed at successive Labour conferences, and their votes weighted accordingly. But by-elections and opinion polls, although not conclusive, hinted that not all trade union members were Labour party voters.

Foot and Healey, in their separate ways, saw what needed to be done. Wrangling over the level of cuts they were prepared to offer the IMF was protracted. In the end, Healey was authorised to offer no more than £1.5 billion of cuts over two years. He was to emphasise the £2 billion of cuts already in the pipeline. Beyond that the party would stand firm. There would be no revisiting the humiliation of the 1968 devaluation, let alone the disastrous crisis of 1948. This was to be an orderly rebalancing, a slowing but not a diversion from a long-term objective that was agreed by all wings of the party and even, a little, by the trade union movement.

In 1978, with the economic crisis not ended but clearly under control and inflation back in single figures, Michael Foot resolved to seek a mandate. But he also knew he lacked the energy to lead his party for another full term, and in truth lacked the appetite too. There were always books to be read, and books to be written. In consultation with the party, less than two and a half years after he won the job for himself, he stood down to allow a successor to win their own mandate.

The only surprise was the party chose not Denis Healey, whose robust defence of the deep cuts in public spending over the past four years had made too many enemies, but Shirley Williams. It was she who, in what amounted to a final triumph for Foot, led the party to a narrow victory over Margaret Thatcher and became Britain's first female Prime Minister.

Prime Minister Healey cuts Thatcherism short

Dianne Hayter

I interviewed Lord and Lady Healey in a sunny Sussex garden on 4 July 2010, just two weeks before Edna's death. Both were in high spirits. Indeed, when I raised the subject of German reunification, Denis serenaded me with the German ditties he used to sing with his old friend Helmut Schmidt, fellow socialist, one-time German Chancellor, and a man with whom he collaborated for nearly forty years. Prime Minister from 1987 until 1992, Healey recounted his recollections of those world-changing days following the 9 November 1989 breach of the Berlin wall.

Healey ruminated over whether he could have played a different role in Bonn in 1989–90, setting Europe on a different course – even while recognising that without his 'eyebrow' thin victory over Michael Foot in November 1980, Labour might not even have been in office at the time. He shook his head, even as he spoke kindly – almost lovingly – about his former deputy leader: 'I think if Michael had become leader instead of me, he might have driven many moderate MPs out of the party by failing to tackle the extreme left and by clinging to unilateralism.' Back then, some observers had predicted that Labour's right might have split off to form a German-style SPD – a left-of-centre Social Democrat party – which would have sent Labour into decades of opposition.

How different from Healey. In his own words: 'I am a socialist who believes that the Labour Party offers the best hope for Britain's future.' The former Prime Minister was made by wars, intense love of his family, pleasure from the arts and culture, a voracious appetite for intellectual knowledge, fluency in foreign languages, hard work – and a passion for politics. Born in the closing stages of the First World War, he spent six years in the army, fighting in north Africa and Italy. This widely read and most erudite of British Prime Ministers knew Europe intimately from his pre-university five-week cycling tour across the continent, ostensibly to see Goethe's *Faust* in Salzburg, but in fact to hoover up political debate with both *Hitlerjugend* and anti-Nazis as well as young Czechs, Dutch and Austrians (and to improve his German to boot). As the Labour Party's international secretary, he witnessed the political transformation of wider Europe, with the shattered continent dividing and rebuilding itself with a West-facing sector and the Moscow-controlled East. Throughout Healey's career, from his 1952 election as MP for Leeds to his position in the highest offices of state, he always played an influential role in shaping European politics.

Sixty-six when he became Labour Party leader, and seventy as he assumed the premiership, Healey possessed the qualities needed for leadership. Clem Attlee once asked Edna (or so she thought) whether Denis was 'a warrior'. About to confirm his reputation as a bruiser, she realised Attlee was asking whether her husband was 'a worrier' as that was no good for a Prime Minister. Far from being a worrier, he was an incurable optimist, with a deep inner exuberance. He had the invaluable gift of making friends and allies among thinkers, and leaders of parties and governments, across the world.

Edna's subtitle to her biography of Emma Darwin, 'the inspirational wife of a genius' would have served equally well as the title for her own autobiography rather than the one she actually went for: *Part of the Pattern*. Perhaps she didn't define the very human Denis as a genius. What she knew was that Healey was not just an intellectual heavyweight but highly pragmatic – and brave – content to do what he believed right, regardless of the effect on his own career. He was fond of the reply of a general to Frederick the Great following an unwelcome request: 'Please tell His Majesty that after the battle my head is at his disposal, but during the battle I propose to use it in his service.' This was Healey's attitude to the Labour Party: at its service, but in ways he believed to be for its own good. Denis also applauded pragmatism, forever quoting his friend Leszek Kolakowski: 'democratic socialism requires … hard knowledge and rational calculation … an obstinate will to erode by inches the conditions which produce avoidable suffering, oppression, wars … hatred … greed and … envy … [This] will do far more to help real people in the real world … than all the cloudy rhetoric of systematic ideologies' (surely a dig at Tony Benn).

In our talk, the former Prime Minister mused on how his record would be assessed by future historians, starting with the composition of his first shadow Cabinet, progressing to his move against the Militant tendency, as he used Labour's traditional spring local government conference in 1981 to follow up his victory in keeping the choice of the party leader in the hands of MPs rather than let it pass to party members and the unions. Wily enough to recognise the strength of Tony Benn's support, he offered the activists four sweeteners. Firstly, an annual re-confirmation of MPs' position (though by David

Owen's favoured One Member One Vote – therefore only half a 'sweetener'); secondly, the presentation of a Pre-Manifesto Programme to conference for endorsement; thirdly, the election of the deputy leader by conference (a clever move as Foot was always bound to win) with the promise of splitting the Prime Minister role from that of party leader once in office, in the German style which he had long admired (meanwhile leaving the premiership in PLP hands); and finally three seats on the NEC for local authority representatives.

These changes drew significant support away from Benn's self-seeking campaign to 'democratise' the party. When the moderate trade unions routed Benn at the 1981 Labour Party Conference (when Benn had challenged his former mentor Foot for the deputy leadership), Healey used one of his most memorable insults: 'To Tony Benn, history is an endless parade, with himself taking the salute.' Benn's political career effectively ended with the melancholy spectacle of the 'would-be proletarian' munching cold fish-and-chips alone in the rain.

Healey's reputation as a political loner stemmed from his hatred (influenced by the 1945–51 government) of the habit of prominent political leaders to have 'a clique of acolytes who never had a good word to say about the leader of a rival clique'. It led to his determination never to encourage a personal clique around him, in contrast to Roy Jenkins and Tony Benn. This nearly cost him the leadership in 1980 but then helped enormously as he put together a broad shadow ministerial team, including (in Barbara Castle's phrase) the 'sane left' as well as popular politicians.

He persuaded Shirley Williams (who had lost her seat in 1979) to go to the Lords as Labour's leader, supported by another new Lord – the left-wing trade unionist Clive Jenkins as Chief Whip (despite the latter's preference for Foot as leader).

Healey knew that the union leader would soon be enveloped by mainstream Labour policies once there. He then set about the PLP which he cajoled – against its better judgement – to elect Bill Rodgers (a formidable organiser) as Chief Whip with left-winger and NEC member Joan Maynard as his deputy (exploiting her 'Stalin's nanny' nickname to intimidate recalcitrant MPs) in a cross-grouping 'dream ticket', while making David Owen shadow Defence Secretary. To add some sparkle to his team, the new leader, having early on decided that Neil Kinnock 'was not lacking in gonads', made the young MP shadow Foreign Secretary (despite his unilateralism, judging that exposure to the realities of world politics would made for fast learning) and distributed other portfolios in recognition of Commons performance rather than debts owed to acolytes. He himself led from the front with some formidable speeches that could thrill the House.

* * *

The first stirrings in Eastern Europe started in Poland with Solidarity, a movement much admired by Healey. He had fought with the Polish Corps for the capture of Ancona on Italy's east coast – close by the shrine of Loreto, a place of Polish pilgrimage – and developed a lasting affection for a nation which had been oppressed over generations by the Germans or the Russians. He had been at the Polish Socialist Party congress in Wroclaw in 1949 when resistance to the Russian Communist hegemony was palpable, and he felt for its democrats then and during a second visit in 1959. He recognised the population's yearning to break free of the communist repression and to 'return to the Europe in which Chopin and Bartók were part of a common civilisation with Bach and Verdi'.

In order to assist Polish Solidarity, while the TUC (still somewhat in hock to Eastern 'trade unions') wavered, Healey joined the maverick Electricians' Union, led by Frank Chapple, which was sending out printing presses and copying machines. He donated a hoard of cameras, film and processing materials, and visited Poland himself to record images. This early support was not forgotten in Poland or elsewhere.

Before the 1982 invasion of the Falklands, the Conservative government was deeply unpopular, with unemployment at over three million (the highest since 1933), manufacturing in decline and inflation high. At the time of the conflict, Labour could not oppose the war, but Healey took maximum advantage of his closeness to the Chiefs of Staff (as former Secretary of State for Defence) and of his war record to get himself flown out to join the Flotilla and then to visit Goose Green after the re-take. He was clearly very supportive of the soldiers, sailors and airmen and, as a former beach master at the Allied invasion of Italy, was particularly sensitive to the dangers – especially from the air – of a seaborne landing force and well aware of the trepidations of the gathering army. His talks with them – officers and men – were later brilliantly recorded by a young airman and became part of the Oscar-winning Falklands film, *Landings from the North*.

But it was his photos – taken throughout that trip and after British rule was re-established – for which he is most remembered. Showcased in the Upper Committee Corridor at the House of Commons, he met both veterans and families – especially the widows – as they viewed this remarkable pictorial record. He signed each book of photos personally for those who came, as only an old soldier (rather than a politician) could. While this was undoubtedly done for noble motives, it was to do former Major Healey no harm come the general election. Would Britain have gone to war had Denis Healey, rather than Margaret Thatcher, been in No. 10 at the time? The former Defence Secretary recalled that in 1977 when there were rumours of a possible invasion, Jim Callaghan had quietly despatched a small naval task force which was quite sufficient to deter the Argentinians. Thus while confident that he would have avoided the conflict, he also knew his duty was to support a successful outcome before moving in on its leader.

Thus in post-Falklands debates, Healey was furious with the government for allowing it to happen, chiding Mrs Thatcher for failing to learn the lessons of thirty years earlier, when the US withdrew troops from South Korea, proclaiming they had no strategic interest there and thus effectively inviting North Korea to invade, just as she had laid the way for the Argentinean invasion. In 1981, one of her ministers had said 'the Falklands are not and never have been part of the United Kingdom', and then (against the protests of the Leader of the Opposition) withdrawn the only naval vessel permanently stationed there – a virtual invitation to the posturing Galtieri, according to Healey. In the post-conflict debates, he was able to admonish her for spending £200 million to defeat the Argentinians rather than the £10 million it would have cost to deter them. It was a war, said Healey, which need never have happened.

As they entered the 1983 election, despite the Falklands, the government was vulnerable. Unemployment was at a post-war high, public services were battered and crime statistics ever worsening. The Conservatives had always feared an election against a Labour Party led by the arch campaigner and proven bruiser, Healey – and now they faced it. His political appetites were sharpened and, having attacked the Prime Minister for having 'cut and run' in an early election, responded to her challenge that he was 'frit' of facing the electorate, with what was to become his infamous remark: 'Come outside!' The cartoonists had a field day, not bettered until the post-Westland debate. (In private company, he referred to it as 'the day the frit hit the shan'.)

Yet Healey's masterly party political broadcast – where he talked through the life chances of a child born under a Tory star, a widowed grandmother in poverty (drawing on Edna's mother who had been widowed early), top-ups needed for health care, a father and brother out of work – was based not on fighting talk but his fears for a future without Labour. He attacked Mrs Thatcher on her intentions regarding the welfare state, where leaked documents on insurance-based health provision, de-indexing of benefits, education vouchers and the introduction of student loans were causing deep unease.

The country, of course, liked Healey. He was fun, he was cheeky and he was a human being even if in an outsize way. He satisfied the middle class with his plans for a multi-lateral defence strategy which would make NATO no longer dependent on first use of nuclear weapons, while appealing to working-class votes with his clear support for strong defence (at a time of continued worries over the Soviet Union and when Healey knew that the rest of Europe was more like to re-arm than dis-arm). Labour was therefore able to hold Derby and David Owen's Plymouth, and do well in defence seats – including Barrow.

Undoubtedly the Falklands and a reviving economy prevented Labour from winning but while Mrs Thatcher, headscarved and triumphant, driving a tank like a modern Boadicea, looked good on TV, it was the pictures of Healey in the Falklands, unashamedly in battle dress, complete with row of medals and with the forces, who more truly represented how the war was seen. Our boys, rather than their leaders, had triumphed over the Argentinians.

Nevertheless, Mrs Thatcher won 42.5 per cent to Labour's 39.6 per cent and the Liberals' 13.3 per cent. A bitter disappointment for Healey who had been confident of victory, along with the pollsters, but progress from the 36.9 per cent of 1979.

There were further headaches for Labour after the election, particularly the 1984–5 miners' strike. However, Healey exploited his deep and longstanding contacts in the unions which came partly from the pragmatism, commitment to working people and intolerance for overblown ideology that they shared. He led endless talks with the various parties, ridiculed Scargill with humour in their many exchanges, and minimised the damage to Labour. He contrived to combine support for mining communities threatened with destruction with condemnation for the incompetent and undemocratic leadership of the NUM – a group of men, he said, who made the First World War donkeys look like stallions.

In 1985 Mrs Thatcher was at the peak of her political powers but then came the Westland crisis and her near-toppling by Heseltine. Healey's astonishing demolition of her was the appetiser for the 1987 election. Unbeknown to him, she had left No. 10 for the Commons exchange insinuating she might not be Prime Minister by that evening. But Healey knew to wound, not kill, as a new incumbent would be a harder target for the election. Nevertheless he was merciless – in turn humorous then rapier-like – while saving some of his best for the prince-in-waiting when, like Mark Anthony, he set about Heseltine-the-Brutus. The Conservative benches squirmed – those who had enjoyed his dissection of Mrs Thatcher loathing his mocking of Heseltine, while in turn Heseltine's detractors gasped at his puncturing of their heroine. (The longer term consequence of his Shakespearean metaphor was that Healey was never again seen in cartoons other than in a toga.)

Healey was in Moscow when Mrs Thatcher called the 1987 election but returned confident of victory. The Prime Minister had been negatively affected by Westland, and there was a growing anxiety towards her shrill personality with its freedom from self-doubt and 'capricious autocracy' in Healey's words. She had long divided the nation, between those admiring 'Good old Maggie' and others pleading 'Ditch the Bitch'.

In the campaign, Healey played to concerns about her style, his election photocalls showing him with children, old people, in crowds but always listening; his humour (to the concern of his handlers) allowed to roam free; his bonhomie evident. It was Father Christmas against the Wicked Witch of the West. Healey would sing 'If she only had a heart', while clicking his metaphorical red shoes, or 'if she only had a brain' as he ran rings round her intellectually. He reminded voters of his own record in restoring a ravaged economy and delivering a sustained period of growing jobs and living standards when Chancellor. The campaign was briefly diverted from its main message by inept attempts to plant stories in the media. Healey instantly dismissed their organiser, a junior party official recruited from TV called Peter Mandelson.

With a comfortable majority, Healey won the general election and immediately began tackling the domestic economic agenda, but also Europe where key intelligence from across the continent, as well as his many discussions with Gorbachev, suggested changes were afoot. Healey had been to the Soviet Union many times – including with Nye Bevan and Hugh Gaitskell thirty years before – and had downed many a glass of vodka with his Russian friends. He despised the fascination that Mrs Thatcher had with Ronald Reagan and her view that

'God separated Britain from mainland Europe, and it was for a purpose'.

He was grounded in European politics, from his bicycling days in the pre-war single Germany, through its literature, art and music to its personalities and potential. He had worked with and admired Ernie Bevin, who had promoted the Council of Europe (to which Denis was later a delegate), engineered the Marshall Plan and influenced the post-war world that Healey inhabited. Denis was well recognised and appreciated in West Germany for the tremendous help he had given (in part due to his complete lack of anti-German feeling) in getting Germany into NATO in the 1950s. He had many political and journalistic friends there, strengthened through his attendance at the Königswinter gatherings, and had met with leading East Germans such as Günter Grass.

Healey's understanding of the Eastern bloc regimes was partly down to his Communist past, but mostly due to his experience of post-war developments, and those of his socialist colleagues who were tortured, imprisoned or killed by the Soviet regimes. He knew of the Communists' antagonism to the capitalist West as well as Russia's post-war hostility, captured on Moscow radio in June 1946: 'This little country [Britain] went to war because its fascist reactionary leaders love war and thrive on war. The attack on Hitlerite Germany was purely incidental.' It is no coincidence that his nom de plume when young had been Blair Winston, testimony to his regard for Orwell.

The new Prime Minister thus made a post-election tour in the summer of 1987 of, effectively, the old Austro-Hungarian empire (Milan, Bratislava, Prague, Dresden and arriving in Budapest by hydrofoil from Vienna) where discussions kept referring once more to 'mittel Europa'. He had met Erich

Honecker in 1986, seeing even in him the desire to visit his birthplace in what was then West Germany. Healey unashamedly showed off to European leaders by quoting long passages – in their own language – from their national poets. He was by far the widest read, and intellectually most sure-footed, of any British Premier.

So as events unfolded in 1989, the Prime Minister was prepared. Unlike his Oxford and Cabinet contemporary Roy Jenkins, who was passionately devoted to the Common Market, Healey had failed to vote for entry in 1971 and was not a 'believer' in it as an institution nor starry-eyed about its role. He might have written Count Coudenhove-Kalergi's words at The Hague in 1948: 'Europe is a means not an end'; that end for Healey was peace and economic prosperity. As he wrote at the time, the UK should only enter when 'our economy is strong ... [and] everything would depend on the terms'. Bill Rodgers was critical of Healey's lack of ballast from a sure, deep, political faith, so unlike Jenkins or Crosland. But that was Healey's strength. He could always pick the route that suited the need. And in 1989, this was to build on Communism's fall.

As the Berlin Wall crumbled, signalling the end of Communism in Europe and the Cold War, Healey was well placed. As an historian, he knew instinctively the symbolism of 9 November for Germany – the anniversary of Kristallnacht. He also recognised immediately that politics changed as the bricks were dismantled. His German was fluent enough for interviews as well as meetings, so he and his Europe Minister, George Robertson, flew to Berlin on 10 November where he undertook a round of TV and radio interviews, welcoming the fall of the Wall wholeheartedly and quickly beginning to float the idea of reunification. Meanwhile Robertson returned to London to front the media coverage, repudiating Mrs

Thatcher's coolness for German reunification, born partly of her personal dislike of Helmut Kohl.

As the weeks passed, the Prime Minister continued to support reunification, emphasising that it would be a new Germany that arose, forming a natural part of Europe. He was clear that was what the German people wanted, a whole but democratic country at peace with its neighbours and contributing to Europe's strength. The whole point of a united Germany was not simply for the German people, but for its integration into a peaceful (and prosperous) Europe. He became the lead European Premier encouraging the westward look to the former Eastern Europe, and invited fellow European Community leaders to the UK, to refocus their thinking to assist the East as it emerged not just from Communism but from low productivity and consumer consumption.

In his discussions with German politicians, he stressed the importance of managing the economy and quickly ensuring real consumption – not simply money in the purse – as well as moving to ensure the entry of the new parts of Germany into the EU by October 1990. But his key achievement was to persuade Kohl not to pledge parity of the East and West Deutschmarks, which he predicted would stall East Germany's economic development and cost the West heavily. Instead, he recommended the establishment of a Euro-German body to bring investment into former East Germany, which would only be possible if wage levels remained attractive (given traditional low productivity). He guaranteed UK assistance for this and undertook to line up the other governments to accept this form of public subsidy. Healey was very aware of the pressures on the US from continuous immigration from Latin America and saw the dangers of free movement within an expanded European Community where the rich West would be a formidable magnet for the youth of the East. So his priority was to ensure a free trade area across the wider Europe with investment being taken to the peripheral areas rather than sucking out the brightest of their graduates and entrepreneurs into the existing golden triangle.

Healey was, by background, a student of Bevin's belief that nations couldn't work together for peace unless they also worked together for prosperity. He had supported the Marshall Plan as a step towards European unity – which he saw as functional co-operation between governments, definitely not federation. He was a long standing opponent of a federal constitution as a means of uniting Europe politically. (He was fond of Bevin's delightfully mixed metaphor: 'when you open up that Pandora's Box, you don't know what Trojan horses are going to come flying out'.) He especially opposed a federal constitution for the former Soviet Union countries which were hostile to central government and anyway would have a strong desire to exercise – some for the first time in generations – their independence and national decision-making powers. So he also opposed further unnecessary integration, favouring a strengthened Council of Ministers rather than a decision-making Commission or European Parliament.

Healey had earlier opposed the EMS and now discouraged the discussion of any monetary union which he considered would jeopardise the growth of the weakest of the Community's members. He emphasised, from his own experience as Chancellor, the difficulty of setting the correct interest rate even for a single nation, let alone a collection of nation states with widely different economies.

So the post-Berlin Wall Europe that emerged – in large part the result of Healey's steering – was as a strong network of independent countries, enveloping the East of Europe but turning away from any thoughts of Cyprus, Malta or Turkey, and shunning talk of a single currency. Free trade rather than harmonisation of working time was the mantra, with free movement of labour being strictly contained. The new Eastern economies thrived under this, fulfilling the Prime Minister's aim.

He retired before everything settled, in 1992, feeling that – at seventy-five – his time was up and the baton should be passed to another.

Prime Minister Kinnock links with the Liberals and abolishes the Lords

Greg Rosen

The Conservative defeat at the 1992 general election was inevitable once Conservative MPs failed to grasp that voters had tired of not just Margaret Thatcher, but Thatcherism as a political creed. John Major tried 'Thatcherism with a Brixton face' but it was found wanting. Neil Kinnock's achievement was to seize the moment after the 1992 election results – and change the political weather. In doing so, the Labour and Lib Dem leaders reshaped British politics for a generation.

The road to the 1992 election became distinctly bumpy for the Conservative government in 1989, when Labour emerged victorious from the European elections. By early 1990, Margaret Thatcher's government had become deeply unpopular. Ignoring Denis Healey's dictum ('when in a hole, stop digging'), Mrs Thatcher had pressed on with the poll tax, precipitating demonstrations of a million people, riots and widespread non-payment. At the same time public services continued to suffer.

On 18 October 1990, the Conservatives suffered a stunning by-election defeat at the hands of the Liberal Democrats in a previously safe seat: Eastbourne. Mrs Thatcher had only weeks earlier dismissed the Liberal Democrats, who had over the previous two years languished in the polls, as a 'dead parrot' in her party conference speech, a mocking reference, after the Monty Python sketch, to their new 'Bird of Liberty' logo. The parrot had bitten back. Conservative backbenchers panicked. Tory Knights of the Shires saw disastrous opinion poll results translating into their own electoral defeat unless Mrs Thatcher was persuaded at least to modify her most unpopular policies.

The Lady was not, however, for turning. Within weeks her deputy Prime Minister, Sir Geoffrey Howe, had resigned, driven to despair by his Premier's increasingly strident anti-Europeanism, and a former Cabinet minister, Michael Heseltine, had challenged Mrs Thatcher for the leadership.

To her great surprise, Margaret Thatcher failed to secure enough MPs' votes to win decisively on the first ballot: only 254 compared to 152 for Heseltine. Since the Conservative Party first introduced a formal system of electing its leader in time for the 1965 leadership contest, the process had been conducted by MPs in successive eliminating ballots and, to be elected, a candidate must have a majority of all voters cast. It was the end for the Iron Lady. The relatively unknown Chancellor, John Major, came through the middle to defeat Heseltine and Foreign Secretary Douglas Hurd, an old Etonian ex-diplomat. Major was thought to be closest to a Thatcher-supported candidate – his meteoric rise to Cabinet had been based largely upon her patronage and he had little independent public standing, in stark contrast to Heseltine. But no one was sure what his real agenda would be.

Initially this was his greatest strength. Voters who had told the opinion pollsters that they would vote Labour to get 'her' out began to talk of giving 'the new man' a chance. There was a feeling of liberation, even though Major's government was nearly identical to the one it had replaced. It took a further

Conservative by-election defeat, in their fourteenth safest seat (Ribble Valley) in March 1991, to convince John Major's government to replace the hated poll tax. From Major's election as Conservative leader in November 1990, until then, the Conservatives had been ahead in the opinion polls.

For Labour, the resurgence of the Lib Dems should have prompted greater pause for thought. On one level it was positive. It meant that the Conservatives were again vulnerable to defeat in rural and Celtic seats that Labour could never hope to gain. But it also foreshadowed the difficulty Labour would still have in achieving an overall majority at the next election under a first-past-the-post voting system.

Some senior Labour figures, such as Robin Cook, acknowledged this. Others, like deputy leader Roy Hattersley, believed that to acknowledge Labour's weakness publicly would be suicidal, and that to win Labour must disavow any likelihood of the need for, or the benefits of, any working relationship with the Liberal Democrats.

The Liberal Democrats remained publicly committed to their policy of 'equidistance', under which they made it clear they would be prepared to sustain either of the main parties in the event of a hung parliament in exchange for a commitment on proportional representation (PR) for elections to the Commons. As talk of hung parliaments intensified in the latter part of the election campaign, Neil Kinnock let it be known at a press conference on Friday 2 April that Labour would like to see other political parties (namely the Liberal Democrats) join the Labour Party Commission on Electoral Systems.

For many voters, the big issue was the economy, and there the Conservative record was threadbare. A decade on from Margaret Thatcher's first recession, an ordeal which, according to the gurus of monetarism, was supposed to have strengthened the British economy, the outlook for most voters bore an unappealing cloak of déjà vu. The recession which began in the autumn of 1990 deepened in 1991, pushing unemployment from 1,600,000 to 2,400,000 by the end of the year. Labour did not hesitate to highlight in its manifesto that 'three thousand men and women lost their jobs on every working day since John Major became Prime Minister. Every week 900 businesses go bankrupt. Every day 200 families lose their homes.' Indeed, Norman Lamont was never perceived by the public as a heavyweight Chancellor.

The majority of newspapers nonetheless remained hostile to a Labour victory. Their attitude, broadsheet and tabloid alike, was epitomised by *The Sun* front page on election day itself featuring Neil Kinnock's head inside a light bulb alongside the headline: 'If Kinnock wins today will the last person to leave Britain please turn out the lights.'

Despite the media campaign against Labour, almost every opinion poll leading up to election day predicted either a hung parliament, in which Labour comprised the largest party, or a small Labour majority of around twenty. Polls on the final days of the campaign gave the Conservative Party between 38 and 39 per cent of the vote, about 1 per cent behind Labour. When the result came through however, it became clear that voters had delivered the first hung parliament since February 1974. This time, the Liberals' successors had performed substantially better, with fifty-three seats. Together with Labour, though not with the Conservatives, they could form a coalition government with a healthy working majority.

John Major resigned, announcing just before midday on the day after polling that 'when the curtain falls, it is time to get off the stage'. He spent the rest of the day at The Oval, watching cricket. Many pundits expected Labour to form an unstable minority government, and Major's advisers argued that were he to remain as Conservative leader in opposition he could well be back in Downing Street within nine months, as Labour imploded under the weight of the onslaught expected from an antagonistic media.

Kinnock seemed to fear no such thing. Power makes some people bloom, and others wilt. Kinnock bloomed. He always had a thin skin for a top politician, but on becoming PM he ceased to have doubts about whether he was up to the job. All those anxieties which lay beneath his surface exuberance seemed to melt away. He stopped worrying about whether some of his colleagues were more academically gifted than he was, and was simply proud of the fact that he was the first Prime Minister since Stanley Baldwin in 1923 to have obtained a degree anywhere other than Oxford – and the first since Campbell-Bannerman in 1905 whose degree came from neither Oxford nor Cambridge. Who gave a fig, now, about Hugo Young's jibe that he had not got a good degree. He could forget the terror that Labour's demise as a party of government might occur when it was under his stewardship. He no longer felt the need to waffle as a means of avoiding questions. His minders had made him put aside the playfulness, the bon mots, the houndstooth suits, but their objective had been achieved now, and he gave himself permission to be his friendly, bouncy, passionate self again, for the first time since he had become leader, just under a decade before. They could call him a Welsh windbag for all he cared. He'd had the last laugh.

It was, ironically, the fires of capitalism that forged the coalition. Margaret Thatcher's government, joining the ERM as it did on the insistence of its Chancellor and over the resistance and reluctance of its increasingly beleaguered Premier, had joined at too high a rate. Kinnock's first action on becoming

Prime Minister, over the weekend following polling day, was to announce the appointment of John Smith as Chancellor, Gordon Brown as Trade Secretary and Lord Eatwell as Minister for the City. In conclave they considered the new government's economic position, and the sustainability of the pledges from Labour's economic team when in opposition to hold the ERM rate.

The folk memory of Labour's misjudgement in 1964 remained strong. Then, Labour's new Prime Minister Harold Wilson, constrained politically by his parliamentary majority of four, decided to prop up the pound at an unsustainable rate. Over the succeeding years the government was to sacrifice public investment and welfare improvements in a vain attempt to avert devaluation. And when it came, it was just as sorry a blow to government credibility as the devaluation of the pound by the Attlee government had been in 1949.

This time, Kinnock, Smith, Brown and Eatwell decided to take a lesson from history and embrace a realignment of the pound within the ERM envelope – devaluation by another name.

Additionally, Kinnock, deputy leader Roy Hattersley and Smith had met Paddy Ashdown, David Steel and Menzies Campbell, Lib Dem shadow foreign and defence spokesmen. Steel as Liberal leader had worked closely with Hattersley and Smith during the 1977–78 Lib-Lab pact, while Campbell was an old friend of Smith's from university days. Few pundits expected Paddy Ashdown and Neil Kinnock to make the leap of faith that they did. Ashdown and Kinnock were not personally close, and precedent (what little there was of it) suggested Labour would prefer to form a minority government rather than a formal coalition. There was, however, enough awareness of the inherent instability of such an arrangement for several senior Labour figures to favour exploring a more formal coalition.

The anticipated media storm over ERM re-alignment never materialised, so astonished was Fleet Street by the announcements which almost immediately followed devaluation. First was the adoption by Smith of one of the Lib Dem manifesto pledges – a calculated and successful measure to reassure wobbling markets – to give the Bank of England independent responsibility for monetary policy, with a requirement to promote price stability. Later that same day came the announcement of a Lab-Lib coalition. Together they pushed the story of the ERM realignment off the front pages. It was the first peace-time coalition since the 1930s and Ashdown, as deputy Prime Minister, together with Menzies Campbell at Defence, Alan Beith at MAFF, and the newly ennobled Bill Rodgers as Lords deputy leader became the first Liberal Cabinet ministers since Archibald Sinclair left office in 1945.

Although Neil Kinnock had a hard time assuaging the egos of Labour ministers offered portfolios of a status below expectations, Gerald Kaufman's apparent demotion from shadow Foreign Secretary to head the new Cabinet ministry for the Arts and Communications proved a great deal less painful – and indeed more successful – than Kinnock's advisers had feared. Jack Cunningham was promoted to Foreign Secretary as a reward for his role in managing the election campaign. He proved an impressive appointment and, with support and encouragement from Paddy Ashdown, played a key role in persuading President Clinton to back the necessary UN action to avoid a potential massacre at Srebrenica and prevent the attempted 1994 genocide in Rwanda. Another unexpected appointment was that of Frank Dobson to Employment, to alleviate concerns in some unions at the influence of the Liberal Democrats within the government. Tony Blair, who had shadowed Employment in opposition and expected promotion, went instead to be Secretary of State for Northern Ireland.

Deputy leader Roy Hattersley demonstrated unexpected enthusiasm for coalition politics with the zeal of the convert. Hattersley's conversion to the cause of electoral reform must rank as one of the swiftest volte-faces in recent political history. Together with the infamous Kinnock/Ashdown joint press conference in the Downing Street garden on the signing of the Coalition Agreement, Hattersley's article in *The Times* setting out the case for the coalition two days later set the tone for its first 'hundred days'. Hattersley wrote:

> Three barriers stand in the way of progress towards co-operation – tradition, tribalism and hubris. A willingness to break with tradition is a radical characteristic. Tribalism – to which I plead guilty in all its manifestations from family to football – ought to be assuaged by the preservation of separate and distinct parties that fight each other during the election and co-operate afterwards. Party leaders who want to strut the stage in independent impotence will have to be swept aside by a members' revolt. Reason should lead the way ... Shirley Williams and I hold almost identical political views ... It is absurd that people like us should struggle to find points of difference and dispute rather than combine to build the sort of society we want to see. My mind has been changed by disappointment. Thirteen years of Thatcherite government has convinced me that under the present voting system, social democracy will never thrive in a society where winning power depends on one party securing an overall parliamentary majority.

Hattersley became Secretary of State for Justice, taking over the combined responsibilities of both the Home Secretary (minus broadcasting) and those of the Lord Chancellor.

At the heart of the Coalition Programme was constitutional reform. Much of the agenda had featured in the manifestos of both coalition partners. The Lib Dems, like Labour, had been enthusiastic advocates of Regional Development Agencies as precursors to elected regional governments, of a Scottish Parliament elected under proportional representation as agreed by the Scottish Constitutional Convention, of a Welsh Assembly, a revived elected Greater London Authority and of a Freedom of Information Act. Both parties also supported an elected second chamber to replace the House of Lords. The main difference of view was over the length and scope of its proposed powers of legislative delay. The Lib Dems preferred wider scope but shorter delaying powers and Labour favoured a narrower scope but the power to force a longer delay. The coalition's constitutional reform agenda, including the introduction of proportional representation in time for the 1994 European Parliament elections, was to fill much of the legislative timetable for the government's first two years in power, not just because of its sheer scale, but because a majority of hereditary peers, determined to avoid their own abolition, decided to ignore the Salisbury-Addison Convention of the 1940s under which the House of Lords undertook not to oppose the second or third readings of any government legislation promised in its election manifesto.

The Commons' decision to abolish the Lords, to ban fox-hunting, and to ratify Maastricht were the three targets for the Democracy Alliance, funded and initially led by Sir James Goldsmith, which, accusing the coalition of 'subverting democracy', marched regularly on the streets of London and established a tented Democracy Village on what had been the grass of Parliament Square. The coalition, they argued, was trampling on Britain's historic traditions. The Scottish Parliament, Welsh Assembly and RDAs were, it was claimed, part of a plan to Balkanise the UK as part of a Federal Europe run from Brussels, and the plan to remove the House of Lords a calculated pre-emptive strike to remove England's remaining protection against that.

Although John Major remained Conservative leader until the election of his successor that July, it was as a lame duck. Shadow Foreign Secretary Norman Lamont laid claim to the leadership of the Eurosceptic right, but was unable to maintain a firm grip on their support. Lamont's leadership rivals from the Thatcherite wing of the party, Peter Lilley and Bill Cash, argued successfully that he lacked the public popularity and support to be suitable as the Conservatives' next leader. Unfortunately, neither did they. To the surprise of some, Michael Heseltine declined to stand – as we now know for health reasons – and backed Kenneth Clarke. Amid an acrimonious campaign Chris Patten, recently defeated at Bath, made a memorable speech to a Tory Reform Group dinner that July in which he argued that Thatcherites needed to take responsibility for the misjudgements of office and the unpopularity and impracticability of the Community Charge, or poll tax as it was generally known. The split that opened up amidst the Conservative right and the unexpected unity of former Heseltine and Hurd supporters around Kenneth Clarke allowed Clarke to triumph by two votes.

Clarke's victory meant an end to the hopes of Eurosceptics that they could harness the Conservative Party to oppose Maastricht, and campaign for withdrawal from the ERM. Clarke moved swiftly to consolidate his grip on the party, appointing key Heseltine lieutenants to control Conservative

Central Office. Appointing Michael Mates as Conservative Party chairman was not a move calculated to appease Eurosceptic or Thatcherite sensibilities, and Mates lost no time in demonstrating his determination to impose his leader's authority, expelling several prominent Young Conservatives for a letter they had penned in *The Telegraph* and suspending the entire executive of the Conservative Collegiate Forum. Unlike the anti-Thatcherites of 1981, Mates could not be accused by his enemies of being 'wet'. More important was the power he exercised through the candidates list, which in the previous general election had shown a markedly Thatcherite flavour. Mates wasted no time in reforming party rules so that local constituency associations were only permitted to select as candidates members of the approved party list, or MPs who were in receipt of the whip. The party leadership could therefore require a rebellious MP (or an MP involved in a scandal) to be deselected. Local members who refused to obey the instructions of Conservative Central Office could have their Association suspended.

When the Maastricht rebellion gathered strength, an irresistible force met an immovable object. Kenneth Clarke argued that the Maastricht Treaty was a Conservative Treaty, and, despite the Social Chapter, should be supported. Precipitating the rebellion was veteran MP Bill Cash, organising the finance and offices to set up the European Foundation and to fund legal challenges to the government. The rebellion had the support of the former Prime Minister Lady Thatcher and former Conservative Cabinet ministers Lord Tebbit and John Biffen. Margaret Thatcher declared in a speech in the House of Lords that she 'could never have signed that Treaty' and that it was 'a recipe for national suicide'. Sir James Goldsmith's Democracy Alliance demanded a referendum on Maastricht and on Britain's membership of the EU.

The Democracy Alliance was not short of MPs for long, for Michael Mates's tough action in suspending the whip from seventeen Conservative MPs who had rebelled in the Maastricht vote in January 1993 – *pour encourager les autres* – proved to be a step too far. Tory MP Nick Budgen's attitude was typical: 'It would be my general feeling that the transference of power to Europe was so important a matter as to require a vote against any organisation and any party that wished to transfer that power,' he said. Suspended from their own party and by no means certain of a political future, the seventeen MPs jumped ship. While some were never likely to be senior Cabinet material; others enjoyed something of a following, and Iain Duncan Smith, Bernard Jenkin, Liam Fox and Alan Duncan were considered potential stars of the Conservative future. Buoyed by the support of the *Daily Telegraph*, the Democracy Alliance stood candidates at both the Newbury and Christchurch parliamentary by-elections during 1993 and 1994 and pulled off remarkable victories at the expense of the Conservative Party which had previously held the seats.

Initially the Democracy Alliance also attracted rhetorical support from the left, veteran Eurosceptic Labour MP Tony Benn endorsing its call for a referendum on Maastricht, and on the coalition's Bills to introduce the Scottish Parliament, Welsh Assembly and the Alternative Vote for the House of Commons. For the coalition, leader of the House Robin Cook reiterated the doctrine of the mandate, and tersely reminded Benn that the government's mandate for constitutional reform and the Maastricht Treaty derived from the very manifesto on which he had stood. Moreover, the referendum on the principle of pooling sovereignty as a member of the EEC had already been held, at Benn's own suggestion, in 1975, and Benn's views had been rejected by the public. Other Labour dissidents were more wary of associating with Goldsmith's Democracy Alliance, especially once it became associated with the pro-fox-hunting direct action movement and the fuel strikes coordinated by road hauliers in protest at John Smith's decision to increase tax on petrol and diesel to pay for greater NHS investment.

At first, many commentators expected an internal Labour revolt against the coalition in general and the introduction of the Alternative Vote (AV) in particular, but just as the Amalgamated Engineering Union (AEU) and the Transport and General Workers' Union (TGWU) leaders Hugh Scanlon and Jack Jones had played a stabilising role during the 1970s so did other key unionists such as Bill Morris, John Edmonds, Bill Jordan and Gavin Laird.

Among Labour MPs, the majority of the opponents of proportional representation seized the opportunity to embrace AV instead. Unlike PR, AV did not jeopardise the single-member constituencies of existing Labour MPs and marginal seats. So long as they retained Lib Dem second preferences, it would make the position of Labour MPs even more secure than first-past-the-post. The Chard speech at which Paddy Ashdown explicitly committed Lib Dems to urging a second preference vote for Labour at the next election helped steady the nerves of some Labour MPs.

By the spring of 1994 it was clear that the growing hysteria of the right-wing press and the Democracy Alliance served only to strengthen coalition support on its own backbenches. The defection of heavyweight former Lib Dem MP Sir Cyril Smith to Michael Meadowcroft's independent Liberal Party in reaction to Ashdown's Chard speech proved to be just a blip on the progressive unity of the government. Moreover, the inter-necine struggle that had broken out within Kenneth Clarke's Conservative Party, and the battle between the Conservatives and the Democracy Alliance made it all the easier for the government to dominate the political landscape.

The European Parliament elections of June 1994, the first conducted under proportional representation, meant that for the first time there were now Lib Dem MEPs. Just as significantly, the old Conservative vote split; with the Conservative Party itself polling a mere 19 per cent and the Referendum Alliance, backed by the full force of the *Telegraph, Mail* and *Sun*, on 21 per cent.

On the weekend following the European elections, the Democracy Alliance organised the largest protest march through London since the Second World War. The *Daily Telegraph*, under the front-page banner headline '407,791 voices cry freedom', devoted its first five pages of Monday's issue to the march and promised an eight-page souvenir supplement the following day. In the week that followed, the Democracy Alliance endorsed 'spontaneous' blockades of petrol stations across Britain organised by the 'Farmers for Justice' movement which demanded red diesel for all rural motorists.

To the government's frustration, the police seemed unable or unwilling to grip the situation and the media were able to splash pictures of chaos all too reminiscent of the grainy pictures of the Winter of Discontent which the latest chaos gave them the pretext to reprint. It got worse: on Wednesday 3 July, the morning that he was due to give a statement in an emergency debate, Chancellor John Smith was rushed to hospital from his London flat. He was declared dead that afternoon. He had had a serious cardiac arrest, said by many to have been induced by the strain of managing the consequences of the fuel protests. During the debate, taken by Gordon Brown in Smith's absence, the Conservative spokesmen were stymied by their reluctance to play politics with a situation they knew had already claimed one life. Several of the Democracy Alliance MPs showed no such qualms, claiming the coalition had caused the chaos itself by imposing unconstitutional policies. Public opinion was divided for months on the issues – and remained so – but the solid centre of the British public supported the government's reluctant decision to use troops to restore order where the police were unable or unwilling to do so.

In the reshuffle that followed John Smith's death, Gordon Brown became Chancellor, being succeeded at the DTI by Margaret Beckett, who in turn was replaced at Social Security by Harriet Harman. Clare Short replaced the ailing Jo Richardson as Minister for Women, Mo Mowlam was promoted to Cabinet to replace the ageing Joan Lestor at DFID. Tony Blair, whose growing success in building a peace process in Northern Ireland was widely admired, turned down the opportunity for promotion in order to finish the job in hand, earning yet more glowing column inches. In 1995, Lib Dem Lord McNally became Minister for Europe, replacing fellow Lib Dem Lord Liddle who became a European Commissioner. In an unusual example of coalition-mindedness, Hartlepool MP and former Labour media supremo Peter Mandelson resigned his Commons seat to go to Brussels as Liddle's Chef-de-Cabinet.

Having struggled to overcome the brickbats for its constitutional reform programme and having largely retained the loyalty of its own supporters, towards the back end of 1994 the coalition's political difficulties mounted on its own side. At the root of it was the tension between tax and spend. Many of the coalition's policies, the constitutional reform programme being a prominent example, were fiscally neutral. Some involved limited transitional or re-organisational costs. These included Labour's pledges to end the deregulation of buses, ban tobacco advertising, encourage healthy diets by introducing clearer food labelling, and encourage unitary local authorities based on districts, and also some shared Lib/Lab policies such as phasing out nuclear power stations and even solely Lib Dem policies such as promoting village 'post and passenger' minibuses, encouraging local authorities to introduce peak-hour car bans, traffic calming measures, car-sharing schemes and further pedestrianisation. The opportunity to implement Lib Dem manifesto commitments to axe the assisted places scheme for private schools and review the charitable status of private schools was similarly affordable and warmly embraced by most of the coalition's Labour backbenchers. Another important and affordable policy implemented by the coalition, included in Labour's 1992 manifesto at the behest of Labour's smaller sister party, the Co-operative Party, was for employees to 'have the opportunity to own collectively a significant stake in the company for which they work, through a democratic Employee Share Ownership Plan (ESOP) or a co-operative', and introduced a new tax incentive 'to encourage companies to establish or extend an ESOP or set up a co-operative'.

Other shared policies, like building a high-speed Channel Tunnel rail link, were more expensive. Transport Secretary John Prescott found his enthusiasm to fulfil this pledge repeatedly blocked by the Treasury, until at the end of 1995 he brokered a privately funded scheme backed by interest-free government loans. Labour's promise to return water to public control and to 'restore public control of the National Grid' involved spending money the government did not, in view of its other commitments, yet have, and the plans were postponed. Other cherished policies, such as the Lib Dems' aspiration to replace the newly introduced Council Tax with a Local Income Tax (and business rates with a business land value tax), were abandoned. It was decided that further upheaval of local government revenue raising so soon after the poll tax disaster would be more trouble than it was worth. Instead, the coalition's local government supremo pushed through legislation to give councils 'a general power of competence, in line with other European countries', so that councils could innovate and develop new services.

While some coalition policies, such as implementing Labour's manifesto pledge to introduce a statutory minimum wage of £3.40 an hour, involved a cost burden that could be passed to the private sector; others, like Labour's manifesto pledge to increase child benefit and the basic state pension, required substantial increases in taxation. This was achieved by abolishing the ceiling on national insurance contributions and introducing a third 50 per cent highest tax band above the 25 per cent basic rate and the existing 40 per cent top rate on incomes above £40,000 (all plans from Labour's manifesto) and implementing the Lib Dem pledge to put a penny on income tax to pay for £2 billion extra investment in education. Additionally, the coalition embraced the Lib Dem manifesto pledge to 'introduce a variety of road-pricing schemes, in which motorists pay a premium to use highly congested roads at busy times of the day' which – to the fury of Lib Dem councillors – John Prescott proved particularly enthusiastic to impose on rural A-roads in Lib Dem-held seats.

Government spending mounted up. The coalition implemented Labour's planned National Recovery Programme (similar to the Lib Dem manifesto plan for 'an emergency programme of investment in the infrastructure and in public works in order to get companies and people back to work, thus reducing unemployment by 600,000 over the next two years') involving temporarily enhanced capital allowances to support business investment, an investment tax incentive for small businesses, the phased release of receipts from the sale of council houses, land and property receipts to allow local authorities to build new houses and improve existing stock, a 'work programme combining three days a week work for the unemployed – paid at the proper rate – with two days' training and job seeking' and money for British Rail to buy new commuter trains. A new National Investment Bank, operating on strictly commercial lines, brought public and private sector together to invest in long-term regional and national infrastructure projects.

The government invested £60 million in the modernisation of Britain's cancer services, using the resources saved by scrapping the Conservatives' tax allowance for private medical insurance. It reduced the shortage of intensive care beds, increased numbers of ambulances, restored free eye tests, and promoted health at work by creating a modern occupational health service within the NHS.

Education Secretary Jack Straw was attacked by Conservative education spokesman Norman Fowler for missing – by three months – the deadline to fulfil Labour's manifesto pledge to 'ensure that within 12 months, no child has to use an outside lavatory' at school. The criticism simply highlighted the failure of the previous Conservative government to tackle the issue at all. But it was soon clear that the money was not available for everything Labour and the Lib Dems wanted to do within one parliament. Labour's manifesto had earmarked the funding from the Conservatives' planned City Technology Colleges to creating 25,000 new nursery places and pledged extra investment in work-based vocational training programmes, in new school buildings and equipment and in reducing primary school classes to under thirty. The money from the CTCs and from the penny on income tax helped the government make progress – but so many school buildings had been left to deteriorate during the Conservative years of austerity that by the time of the 1996 general election there were still many buildings needing renewal and refurbishment.

The coalition's pledges and implied commitments needed more money than had been raised by John Smith's tax and national insurance rises and the new Chancellor Gordon Brown was determined not to repeat the mistakes of previous governments and squeeze more out of the economy than it could bear. This gave rise to the issue that put the coalition under its greatest strain: the controversy over university funding. Under the thirteen years of Conservative government, universities had been starved of cash, academic salaries had been filleted and student support reduced.

Roy Jenkins, leader of the Liberal Democrats in the Lords, declined to serve in government. Instead, being the Chancellor of Oxford University, Jenkins was persuaded to lead the National Committee of Inquiry into Higher Education, which became known as the 'Jenkins Commission'. It was the largest review of higher education in the UK since the Robbins Committee in the early 1960s and its main report, published in early 1996, made ninety-three recommendations concerning the funding and expansion of universities and the maintenance of academic standards.

Labour's manifesto had pledged to replace the Conservatives' student loan scheme with 'a fairer system of student grants and targeted help for housing and vacation hardship', a pledge that in the light of the Jenkins Commission recommendations proved a hostage to fortune. The Lib Dem manifesto was similar in tone. It had promised to 'abolish student loans and restore student entitlement to housing benefit and income support', and ultimately replace them with a 'Student Income Entitlement and a Student Allowance to which all students, both full- and part-time, will be eligible'. Other parts of the Lib Dem manifesto had committed to 'increase the number of students in higher education to two million by the year 2000' while ensuring that 'as numbers rise, quality does not suffer', and 'a Pay Review Body for academic and non-academic staff to halt the brain drain' implied that university salaries would be boosted. This proved to be an impossible circle to square. Instead, reflecting the interests of academe in general and Oxford University dons in particular, Jenkins' report urged a swift and substantial increase in university funding paid for by students. This entailed a shift from undergraduate tuition being funded entirely by grants from the government to a mixed system in which tuition, supported by low interest government loans, was paid for by students. This was in addition to the complete substitution of student loans for grants. Given other government priorities, such as the Lib Dems' commitment not just to boosting schools funding but also to ensure 'an annual real increase' in NHS funding 'to replace the underfunding suffered by the Health Service under the Conservatives' and to 'invest more in renovating and constructing new health service buildings', it is perhaps not surprising that Jenkins reported as he did. Nevertheless it caused a great deal of political pain for the government.

Not only were many Labour and Lib Dem activists profoundly opposed to the concept of top-up tuition fees, but many coalition MPs had won their seats on the back of student votes. The Prime Minister was reluctant to accede to the Jenkins Commission's recommendations. Kinnock had famously once said that he was the 'first Kinnock in a thousand generations' to be able to get to university and he did not want to be the one to pull the ladder from under future generations. But there seemed to be no fiscal alternative.

The decision of the coalition to accept the Jenkins Commission recommendations caused a storm of opprobrium. Despite the formidable campaigning machine built up by Labour's Youth Development Officer Tom Watson, the 'No Way Woy' campaign saw Labour lose control of the National Union of Students in 1996 for the first time in decades, and, more significantly for parliamentarians in marginal seats, suffer a haemorrhaging of support on university campuses. Worse still, NUS and university students unions endorsed a tactical voting campaign to evict coalition MPs in the twenty or so seats where the student vote could swing the election. The coalition MPs pointed out that the Conservative Party had abolished grants in the first place and was unable to guarantee to reverse tuition fees. The real threat to coalition MPs came from the Democracy Alliance, which pledged to pay for the abolition of tuition fees and re-introduction of grants from the money saved by renegotiating the UK's contribution to the EU. If other EU members would not agree to such a reduction, they said, then the UK could simply refuse to pay or withdraw from the EU entirely and focus trade instead on America and the Commonwealth.

The 1996 general election superficially mirrored 1992 in that it again produced a hung parliament with only the Lib Dems and Labour capable of forming an overall majority. It saw the coalition reap the benefits of the Alternative Vote and both Labour and Lib Dem candidates recommending second preferences for each other. Despite Labour's vote falling to 37 per cent and the Lib Dems to 17 per cent, both parties (and the SNP and Plaid in Scotland and Wales) made gains at the expense of the Conservatives, who lost forty-three seats. The

Democracy Alliance won thirty-seven seats. Twenty were in student-influenced seats such as Oxford West, Cambridge, Sheffield Hallam and Brighton, but others were in rural areas where the former Conservative MP, suspended by his or her own party, had held on. During the campaign, the endorsement of Conservative Peers such as Lord Tebbit and Lady Thatcher – who enthusiastically pointed out to voters in university seats that, unlike the coalition, she had not introduced tuition fees – clearly made an impact. As Peers they were, moreover, impossible for Conservative Central Office to 'de-select'.

Coalition negotiations following the 1996 election proceeded swiftly. Neil Kinnock remained in Downing Street and the Cabinet was re-appointed much as before, with the addition of a couple of newcomers on the Labour side: Alan Milburn at Energy and Stephen Byers at Education. The most significant aspect of the new coalition agreement, much of which embodied a continuation of the unfinished business of 1992–96, was to have a referendum on changing the Commons electoral system to proportional representation. Kinnock had refused to commit the government to introducing PR on the grounds that most of his MPs and the main union leaders were against it. Ashdown accepted the difficulty, and proposed the referendum as a way out of the impasse, for his own activists demanded it. Moreover, unlike AV, there had not previously been a parliamentary mandate for it.

Initially, many Labour sceptics of proportional representation anticipated that the referendum, scheduled for the summer of 1998, would produce a 'No' verdict and close down the issue. The Conservative Party and most of the right-wing press had historically opposed PR and the coalition's own popularity was waning. The government's extra investment, while clearly delivering improvements to many public services, had not improved education standards or cut unemployment as much as the coalition had hoped or voters, judging by the waning Labour and Lib Dem ratings, had expected.

The decision of both the right-wing press and the Conservative Party to back the Democracy Alliance's call for a 'Yes' vote in the PR referendum changed all that. Taking as their cue Winston Churchill's argument in 1931 that proportional representation was better for Conservative politics than the Alternative Vote, they saw that PR could provide a mechanism to break apart the Lib/Lab entente. The temptation to support PR was impossible for Lib Dems to resist. By a whisker they won the referendum, and the seeds were sown for the destruction of Kinnock's premiership.

The tension between the competing demands of tax and of spend had continued to eat away at the coalition. This manifested itself in growing dissatisfaction among public sector workers with levels of pay. Labour's manifesto commitment was to 'halt the deterioration which has taken place in the pay and conditions of many public service workers – often through pay settlements which have been arbitrarily imposed'. This was taken by many activists within the unions to mean an implied promise of year-on-year real-terms pay increases, to compensate them for the real-terms pay cuts that many had suffered under the lean years of Thatcherism. They did get pay increases, but with inflation up as a consequence of the devaluation, the pound in their pocket was squeezed and many employees felt short-changed. Militant activists argued that the coalition was betraying Labour's pledges and won votes at union conferences for a tough line on pay negotiations with the government and for industrial action to 'force Labour to keep its promise'. A growing belief among voters in the south of England that taxes were too high and that too much of the coalition's investment went to 'waste', a belief fostered by the daily stories of waste, red-tape and incompetence in the public sector on the pages of the tabloid press and Conrad Black's *Telegraph*, also took its toll on coalition popularity.

At the general election in June 2000, held under proportional representation, Labour slipped to 32 per cent and the Lib Dems to 14 per cent. Kinnock resigned as Prime Minister immediately, as John Major had done eight years before, gambling that his opponents would be unable to cobble together a deal. It surprised those who had observed the feuds over Maastricht that had divided them seven years earlier, but the temptation of office is a powerful elixir, and Kenneth Clarke found that Iain Duncan Smith's Democracy Alliance was prepared to form a coalition government with his Conservative Party. Their joint purpose was to reduce waste in government and cut spending and tax. Considerable credit was given by the media to the skill of their 'fixers', for just as Charles Clarke and Neil Stewart for Neil Kinnock in 1992 and Alan Leaman for Paddy Ashdown were instrumental in making the original coalition work, so were David Cameron and Nick Clegg for Iain Duncan Smith and Kenneth Clarke after 2000.

The charisma and energy of Labour's new leader, Tony Blair, whose achievement and reputation in securing peace in Northern Ireland enabled him to defeat Gordon Brown in the leadership election that followed Kinnock's retirement in 2000, helped evict the Clarke-IDS coalition from office at the 2004 election, after only one term. Whether Cameron and Clegg, now leaders of their respective parties, will be able to defeat Tony Blair's New Labour coalition at the 2012 election, and what role might the Lib Dems play, is for future historians to judge.

Prime Minister Smith
looks to Brussels, not Washington

Francis Beckett

By the time John Smith retired in 2002, aged sixty-four, he had established a mastery over the Labour Party not seen since Attlee. Smith led Labour for ten years, from 1992, and was Prime Minister for the last five of them; by the time he left, he was so firmly in control that he could easily have had another five, perhaps ten, years at the top, if it were not for his suspect heart.

Yet it had not always been so. That mastery was established in government, not in opposition. Labour had come so close to forming a government under Neil Kinnock at the 1992 general election that its top echelon could smell the power, could almost touch it. But the cup, held tantalisingly just out of reach ever since Margaret Thatcher's first victory in 1979, was cruelly snatched from them at the last moment.

To say that politicians like Gordon Brown, Jack Straw and Tony Blair were hungry for power in 1992 doesn't quite cover it. It was not the sort of hunger you feel when you've gone without lunch, but the sort you feel when you missed out on the last crust of dry bread and sip of water three weeks ago.

These men looked to the new leader to deliver them power before the lack of it drove them mad. They had never sat in the back of their own ministerial limousine, while Smith – as they pointed out grimly in endless meetings of cabals inside cabals – had. If Labour never held power again, John Smith would have a career to look back on which included being Trade Secretary and a Privy Councillor. The baby boomer generation of politicians around Smith, who had grown up in the radical sixties, were terrified that their time would come and it would go, and that by the time Labour's turn did at last come again, they would be old men and women, displaced by sharp-toothed children of the eighties.

So, right from the start, they looked at Smith and worried. He seemed to have little appetite for changing the Labour Party beyond the far-reaching reforms already established under Neil Kinnock.

Nothing was done about Clause Four, which seemed to say that Labour would nationalise everything. Smith replied complacently that no one thought Labour was going to nationalise everything, so what did it matter? But, the Browns and the Blairs shouted despairingly, that missed the point. The task was to draw attention to it so as to dump it, and show how determined the party was to jettison everything it had done before.

The baby boomer politicians urged frantic action to distance their party from outdated notions of equality, and pointed out that many of these notions were not far short of 100 years old, dating back to strange folk in frock coats with odd-sounding names like Keir Hardie. But John Smith came back to work after his second heart attack in 1994 apparently more certain than ever that everything was going to be all right, just so long as Labour remained steady. That heart attack, it was whispered in the committee corridor, might have killed him. Another missed opportunity, they muttered grimly.

Smith did force through far-reaching changes that reduced trade union influence in Labour's affairs, but he did not seem to want permanent conflict with the unions. He never seemed to realise that attacking the unions was a God-given means of showing the middle classes that he was on their side. He suggested that trade unions were a part of the body politic which a government ought to consult every now and again, and Tony Blair recalls in his memoirs how he had to stop himself from exploding at a meeting of the shadow Cabinet. Smith even seemed rather at home on the annual visits to the Trades Unions Congress which he insisted on paying. He was still on fancy-a-drink terms with John Edmonds, the leader of the GMB union, who might at any moment embarrass Labour by putting in a pay claim which the *Daily Mail* could attack.

Nothing was done about the anarchic system by which any constituency Labour Party or trade union could get its pet motion on to the annual conference agenda. Smith seemed to think the grassroots members making themselves heard wasn't entirely a bad thing. So Labour's conference was still capable of doing something unscripted and unexpected, and Smith did not show what many of his shadow Cabinet colleagues considered the proper zeal to homogenise it. They could not understand why Smith's appetite for constitutional Labour Party reform seemed so easily sated.

They called themselves 'the modernisers' and they worried themselves sick.

Hardly a day went by without a coded attack on Smith from one or other of the modernisers, and by 1997, to insiders at any rate, his grip on the leadership looked distinctly shaky. But Smith's massive 99-seat majority in the June 1997 general election – the second-highest in Labour's history – silenced his critics. Privately, the modernisers claimed it could have been twice as big if their prescriptions had been adopted, but even if true, it did not seem to matter: ninety-nine was good enough for most people.

It was certainly enough for Smith to take a few instant decisions without much controversy, such as cancelling a now long-forgotten proposal to build a vast round shed in Greenwich, south London, which the Conservatives had planned as a symbol for the millennium, and for which nobody could think of a use.

But if Smith's own party ceased to be a danger to him, the Conservatives became so more quickly than anyone could have expected, given how split they were under John Major's leadership. This was traceable to the influence of the luckiest MP in that parliament, Michael Portillo. He hung on to his Enfield seat – and therefore his right to stand for the vacant Tory leadership – by just a handful of votes after three recounts. Portillo rattled the Prime Minister when, as opposition leader, he went soft and liberal and cuddly, occasionally sniping at Smith from the left. Portillo even argued that the battle between left and right was out of date, and talked about something called a 'Third Way'. Labour's Home Secretary, Tony Blair, was put up to attack it – a clever choice, because he was the Cabinet's chief moderniser and might have been expected to find it attractive. Blair, in an uncharacteristically irritable speech, called the Third Way 'vacuous'.

Yet Labour was at times close to panic over Portillo's unexpected bid to be the Tories' Neil Kinnock. Blair was known to be frustrated at Smith's laid-back reaction. To the Prime Minister, however, Portillo's volte face simply confirmed his instinct that Labour needed to be true to itself as the party that used state power to redistribute wealth – a road down which Labour could go much further than Portillo could hope to follow.

So the Chancellor, Gordon Brown, was persuaded, against his instincts, to agree to 'hypothecation' – earmarking certain taxes specifically for schools and hospitals. Labour's pollster Bob Worcester – now back in favour after being excommunicated by Peter Mandelson in the Kinnock years – told Smith that the voters were willing to pay higher taxes if they could be sure the money was going to health and education.

The Education Secretary, Ann Taylor, tore down the distinctions between state schools. She ensured that every school was funded at the same level, and that none could select the brightest pupils. She made local authorities the engine of her schools policy. Relying heavily on a Prime Minister who thought education in the rest of the country should be run as it was in his native Scotland, she announced: 'There will be no failures, and no schools designed for failures.' But, to the disappointment of the left, private schools remained untouched – a task for her successor, she said mischievously.

The Health Secretary, David Blunkett, tore down the NHS 'internal market', embarked on a hugely expensive modernisation programme, and grandly announced the end of health service rationing (a promise, it has to be said, which the government has not been able to keep). The Agriculture Minister, Gavin Strang, disdaining the once-powerful farming and landowning lobby, forced farmers to increase the low wages paid to their workers, and put himself at the head of the movement to ban fox-hunting, which was passed into law just before the 2001 election.

The Transport Secretary, Ken Livingstone, was Smith's bravest appointment, or his stupidest, depending on your point of view. So delighted was Livingstone with his Cabinet status that, to Smith's consternation, he declined to return to London politics after the government had created a new structure of regional and local government, restoring real power to great cities such as London. The task of using the Greater London Authority's extensive tax-raising powers to transform the capital's transport and education went instead to Frank Dobson.

Livingstone believed that Dobson's proposal to ban cars from the centre of London was a step too far, but after a magisterial rebuke from Smith's spokesman, the unflappable David Hill, he wisely kept his own counsel. The Prime Minister, said Hill, believed that 'there is no point in regional government if central government keeps stepping in and telling it what to do'. Livingstone hastily retreated to what he does best, upsetting the airlines by refusing a third runway at Heathrow, upsetting the car lobby with motorway tolls, and upsetting the left by allowing public–private partnerships to bring in some capital for his renationalisation of the railways.

The 1997–2001 parliament was, on the whole, a successful one for Labour. Some referred to it as 'the Smith revolution', but the Prime Minister himself observed more modestly that 'there were some changes which badly needed making, and we made them'. It was enough, anyway, to get the government re-elected in 2001, though with a substantially reduced majority.

Smith's post-election Cabinet changes were the most far-reaching he had undertaken. The Foreign Secretary, Jack Cunningham, the surprise success of the first term, was at last pushed into the 'elder statesman' role he had resisted for so long. When he was summoned to Downing Street, he pleaded that he was only a year younger than Smith himself, but was met, according to reports, with Smith's kindest and most intransigent smile.

That interview was nothing to the torment Smith inflicted on his fellow Scot and protégé Gordon Brown, who became probably the most reluctant Foreign Secretary in British history, watching with quiet fury as Robin Cook sat in his old chair at the Treasury and moved with what Brown regarded as imprudent haste into the euro.

But to Brown and Cook, there was a political logic in joining the euro zone. They saw it as much more than an economic decision. It was nothing less than a statement about who Britain was in the world, and where she stood. Smith was more of a European than many of his colleagues; and much less of an Atlanticist. He did not warm to US President George W. Bush, and Bush saw in the Prime Minister all the vices he attributed to louche, lazy, pinkish Europeans.

Smith was happy, after 9/11, to send British troops to Afghanistan, but he drew the line at committing himself to war in Iraq. On this issue, Britain made common cause with the French, to Bush's fury.

Brown as Foreign Secretary could not change the essence of the policy established by Smith and Jack Cunningham, even though he was much more of an Atlanticist than the Prime Minister. The government had its eyes firmly on Brussels rather than Washington, and that was that. Smith had proved the only Prime Minister since 1945, with the single exception of Edward Heath, who looked East and not West.

But Brown did bring a new tone of voice. The reward for being deprived of the Treasury was far greater independence from Downing Street than is granted to most foreign secretaries, and it fell to him, as far as it was possible, to keep the Americans on board. In his last three years in Downing Street, John Smith never once visited Washington.

And Brown was still, as far as anyone could see, the only possible successor. If you had watched closely as MPs processed to the House of Lords for the Queen's Speech at the start of the 2002 session, you might have spotted a faint smile playing around his granite features. He had the important, though double-edged, support of his old friend Tony Blair, by 2002 out of the running for the top job because his dislike of what he privately dismissed as 'the Smith project' became common knowledge. Blair had been relegated to Education, where he was not permitted to change any of Ann Taylor's policies.

Brown also had the tacit support of the Prime Minister, or so he believed. Though it is widely assumed that he backed Brown, the PM, even over the lemonade and angostura bitters that were the nearest his doctors would now allow him to get to alcohol, kept his own counsel. When Smith did announce his resignation, he gave Brown a week's notice before telling the rest of the Cabinet. At the time, Brown thought only he had been given this head start. But as time went on, and memoirs started to come out, it slowly became clear that another key figure had been given advance warning, too, and this explained how another candidate managed to be ready when the announcement came.

Politics often has a cruel way with front runners. The chronically divided left unexpectedly buried its growing distrust of the newly promoted Environment Secretary, Gordon Brown's old nemesis Ken Livingstone, and paved the way for ten years of municipal socialism.

Prime Minister David Miliband creates a Lab-Lib coalition

Peter Beckett

At the end of 2010, Prime Minister David Miliband's most pressing concerns should have been the deepest winter freeze for decades and the unprecedented series of leaks from the US State Department, ruthlessly plastered over the internet by WikiLeaks and printed across the front page of each day's *Guardian*. They were disturbing, even if they did not do as much damage to him as to others. He might have preferred the world not to know that he'd been described by the US Ambassador as 'thoughtful, eloquent, and knowledgeable to the point of geekiness'. Some of his decisions had been given an unwanted airing and his weakness in Cabinet had been underlined, too.

In fact, none of that was at the front of his mind, for he had an unwanted general election on his hands.

And it came at a bad time. He faced an opposition in better shape than it had been for two decades – a rejuvenated Conservative party led by a rejuvenated William Hague, looking capable of claiming an overall majority in the wake of the coalition Lib-Lab government's demise.

How had it come to this? Looking back now, with the benefit of hindsight, we can see that the seeds of his government's destruction were sown the day he narrowly beat Gordon Brown to the job the son of the Manse had worked and waited for all his life.

Brown had been a thorn in Miliband's side ever since Miliband had pipped him to the leadership in 2007. Their relationship, never good, had become ever more strained with each policy decision, but the final fracture came in the wake of proposed cuts to Building Schools for the Future (BSF), which involved slashing the programme's budget by almost four-fifths.

This proved to be the straw that broke the camel's back. Brown and Ed Balls saw BSF as their brainchild, the sort of programme they had come into politics to make happen. The Lib-Lab coalition government, formed after the 2007 election which left Labour with the advantage but without a majority, was already divided over the proposed cuts to public spending that Miliband had insisted were necessary to tackle the deficit. The government's struggle to contain the divisions within the Cabinet room and private chats in No. 10 between Miliband and Brown suffered a serious blow when Miliband was pictured in public with a black eye. No one ever commented on it officially, but the Lobby was alive with rumours that it was caused by a stray government BlackBerry.

The Liberal Democrats, already unhappy with the brutal austerity package Miliband was asking them to support, smelled blood. Their leader, Chris Huhne, had reportedly given Miliband a list of demands without which the Lib Dems would withdraw their support for the government, including Building Schools for the Future. When the PM made it clear that he wouldn't be held to ransom, Huhne began talks with the Brownites, culminating in the announcement that shocked the British political world.

Rumours of Brown's impending resignation had been

circulating for days. Brown called a press conference on 30 November. By the time the Lobby gathered to hear him, they had a rough idea of what he would announce. He said:

> I have supported the Labour Party all my life, and I've always been certain that it was the best force for the advancement of the interests of hard working families in Britain. But the party has announced that it is to cut the much needed investment in our country's schools, while letting the banking system which caused this recession off the hook. This is not what I came into politics to do. And that is why, with a heavy heart, I announce today that I can no longer stay in the government.

* * *

It was all a far cry from the heady early days of the elder Miliband's premiership. Back in 2007, when Tony Blair finally yielded to the insistent demands from increasingly large sections of the Parliamentary Labour Party that he should resign, the name of Blair's successor was at first thought to be a foregone conclusion. Gordon Brown had it wrapped up, said conventional wisdom.

Of course, there were still Brown's diehard enemies, who would fight to the last ditch to prevent it. John Hutton, John Reid and Charles Clarke were simply keen to see anyone but Brown get the premiership. They argued that a Brown government would become unpopular because of its leader's apparent lack of communication skills and his awkward manner on television, and they whispered in the Commons corridors that they thought the Chancellor had what they described darkly as 'emotional problems'. The dreaded phrase 'psychological flaws' was heard again in hushed tones wherever two or three Labour MPs gathered together. But they were having to resign themselves to the inevitable. None of them any longer carried enough credibility to stand for the leadership. Their only hope was a Miliband candidacy and David Miliband's own brother, Ed, privately told him that even he would support his old mentor Gordon Brown if it came to it. Miliband saw himself being wielded like a weapon in the hands of a few ageing diehards and eventually going down with them. The prospect was not appealing to a young, able politician for whom everyone predicted a brilliant future.

What changed his mind was Tony Blair. It was one thing for the Blairites to urge him on but quite another for the man himself to join in. Blair convinced Miliband that his time had come. Blair told Miliband he believed Gordon's time came and went when Neil Kinnock resigned as leader in 1992. Brown, said Blair, should have challenged John Smith for the leadership then. He would have had the support of the modernisers, including Blair himself. When Brown failed to do that, he showed himself unfit to lead, said Blair. That was the harsh message he'd had to convey to his one-time friend all those years ago, he told Miliband; Brown had never forgiven him.

Now, in 2007, it was Miliband's moment, just as surely as it had been Gordon Brown's moment in 1992 and Tony Blair's in 1994. Take it now, urged Blair. If you wait your turn behind Gordon, you will find that when he goes it will be for someone else, maybe Yvette Cooper, maybe Ed Balls, maybe even Miliband's own younger brother Ed. Seize your moment, said Blair, and I will strain every muscle to help you succeed. And Blair was as good as his word.

Miliband's victory in the 2007 leadership election, in which only he and Brown stood, came on a wafer-thin margin. Brown had the support of the Unions, and the Parliamentary

Party was fairly evenly split. It came down to the rank and file members. The bitterly disappointed and angry Gordon Brown reluctantly accepted his old job, and trudged back disconsolately to the Treasury. Ed Miliband, David's brother, was deputed as Chief Secretary to keep an eye on Brown and to try to reconcile him to the eclipse of a lifetime's dream.

Even more dramatic than Miliband's victory were the first months of his premiership: the bailout of subprime mortgage lender Northern Rock, terrorist attacks at Glasgow Airport and a foot and mouth outbreak were early challenges that defined his premiership. His competent handling of all three and his ability to pass on the blame for the brewing financial storm to Brown, his Cabinet foe, helped the Labour Party rise ahead in the polls – the 'Milibounce', as the media called it.

But Miliband's election had re-ignited the Blair–Brown wars with a vengeance. His support in the party was strong, but the Brownites were mobilising. Their man had now been cheated twice, and their wrath was terrible. Their mood was not at all lightened by what seemed to be a sort of jaunty triumphalism in Blairite circles. Charles Clarke in particular was not able to disguise his pleasure at Brown's discomfiture. His vast, grim bulk seemed suddenly cheerful in a way that no one could remember since the day he had masterminded Neil Kinnock's victory in the leadership election back in 1983, and on the day of the result he revived an old joke from his student days. 'It's a great day for the race' he told friends. 'What race?' they asked. 'The human race' shouted Clarke, and almost seemed to skip away to share his joy with yet another MP.

When Labour MPs are at each other's throats, there is only one thing the leader can provide to effect some sort of temporary truce. So, in his first leadership speech at the 2007 Party Conference, Miliband called a snap election, to be held in November, arguing (rather speciously, some thought) that a new leader needed a new mandate.

A coalition government was a possibility from the start of the campaign, because neither Labour nor the Conservatives looked like winning an overall parliamentary majority. Labour's 'Milibounce' was already starting to subside, and the new Conservative leader, David Cameron, could no longer rely on his youth to give him an automatic advantage, as he could have done had he fought Blair. So what the Lib Dems did was of crucial importance, and here a part of Miliband's strategy misfired. He had hoped he would catch the Lib Dems unaware, for they had just deposed Menzies Campbell as their leader and were in the midst of a leadership contest when the general election intervened. They had to enter it with an acting leader, Vince Cable, who was not even a candidate for the leadership, and who, as a man in his sixties, carried all the problems that had done for Menzies Campbell. But Cable, unexpectedly, was able to score some big hits on the economy.

The 2007 election saw the first televised leaders' debates. Cable was able to win all three convincingly, eloquently running rings around both Miliband and David Cameron on the economy, and helping the Lib Dems to a handsome total of ninety-two seats. His age – which had been his predecessor Menzies Campbell's undoing – proved a positive advantage in the election hothouse, for he sounded reassuringly mature beside the two young men in charge of the two major parties.

Labour retained its advantage, though not its overall majority, gaining 274 seats with the Conservatives on 249. Cable played a shrewd game during negotiations that lasted only a few days, securing himself the Treasury, Nick Clegg the Home Office, Chris Huhne Energy and Climate Change, and Simon Hughes Transport. This would prove fatal for Clegg's leadership aspirations, forcing him to take a cautious tone over the Liberal Democrats' opposition to identity cards and enhanced detention powers for terrorist suspects. His Labour colleagues would not let him tamper with either. It smelled of betrayal to the Liberal Democrats, and helped ensure a Huhne victory in the leadership contest in December.

On the opposition benches, the Conservative Party, never tolerant of failure, forced out its leader David Cameron, amidst accusations that he had cost them the election by being too timid about enunciating the true Tory philosophy.

A disgruntled Brown, forced out by Liberal demands for the Treasury, reluctantly accepted the Foreign Office. His principal disciple, Ed Balls, was given the Department for Children, Schools and Families, a position he had long cherished, and told to keep quiet and stand for the leadership next time around.

Brown's anger, for once, was not the most combustible substance around the Cabinet table. Liberal leadership hopeful Nick Clegg fumed as Chris Huhne defeated him by pointing to Clegg's betrayal on those touchstone Liberal issues of identity cards and 42-day detention. Then, when the Liberal leadership campaign was all over, Miliband set up the Prescott Commission on Civil Liberties, headed by the UK's new envoy to the Council of Europe, and told it to report in a month. Prescott recommended that ID cards and 42-day detention proposals be dropped. It was a remarkable U-turn for the man himself which was not lost on the new Conservative leader, William Hague – and it permanently wiped the smile from the boyish face of Nick Clegg. He was being given permission to tell the world that he had always believed passionately in these proposals when it no longer had the power to do him any good.

But the financial storm Northern Rock had presaged the previous year was still brewing. Confidence in the markets was low, commodities and gold sky-rocketed, and banks across the world slowly began to admit that falling house prices and the steady rise in unemployment were having a serious effect on their balance sheets. The market for inter-bank loans eventually revealed that the situation was worse than most had suspected: banks were too scared even to lend to each other.

The government had no choice but to bail out a large proportion of the British banking system – most couldn't even borrow enough money at the end of the day to meet their capital requirements. HBOS was sold to Lloyds in a transaction that was more like a shotgun wedding, and RBS became more than four-fifths owned by the British taxpayer.

The Lib Dems in Cabinet argued furiously that some kind of recovery package was needed. Confidence in the resilience of the economy was at an all-time low with speculation about the next great depression looming high on the horizon. But ratings agencies had hinted at downgrading British Sovereign debt for some time following the banking crisis, and Miliband worried that the country couldn't afford a hike in the rate it borrowed money at. Without an election for another four years, Miliband reasoned that cutting now would give wriggle-room for spending closer to an election.

Labour ministers briefed anonymously that there was likely to be a 'bonfire of the quangos', that University tuition fees were likely to rise and that every department would need to find 'efficiencies' from somewhere. The situation continued to rile Gordon Brown, the increasingly embittered Foreign Secretary, who found that much of the work he had done as Chancellor was being undone, and that his time in office was being subtly blamed for the need to do it. He became an increasingly reticent Foreign Secretary, making far fewer trips abroad than Miliband had done when he was in the job, and briefing against the PM and his cabal of advisers on an almost daily basis.

The loss of either the Brownites or the Lib Dems would have been deeply dangerous for the government. The loss of both at once was fatal.

The government responded to Huhne's withdrawal of support and Brown's resignation the only way it could, by calling an election for February, with the warring parties to remain as a 'lame duck' coalition until then.

With the Liberal Democrats looking certain to increase their presence in Parliament, possibly even surpassing that of the Labour Party, all eyes are on the Conservative leader William Hague. If he can win an outright majority, he will become the party's hero. If he fails, disgruntled Cameronites are likely to strike – but as we write, failure does not look like a live possibility.

Contributor biographies

Stephen Bates is a senior correspondent for *The Guardian*. He has reported on Westminster politics at various times for the BBC, the *Daily Telegraph* and *The Guardian*. He studied History at Oxford.

Phil Woolas was Labour MP for Oldham East and Saddleworth for thirteen years and Minister of State under both Tony Blair and Gordon Brown. A former President of the NUS, he was a TV journalist and producer for TVS, BBC's *Newsnight* and *Channel Four News*. For seven years he was Head of Campaigns and Communications at the GMB trade union.

Hugh Purcell is a writer and broadcaster specialising in twentieth-century British and Empire history. His books include *The Last English Revolutionary*, a biography of Tom Wintringham and *After the Raj*, about the last stayers-on and the legacy of British India. He was executive producer of the BBC TV series *Roads to War*, a country-by-country approach to the causes of the Second World War, which first brought to his mind the idea of his piece on Halifax as Prime Minister.

Nigel Jones is a historian, biographer and journalist. A former deputy editor of *History Today* and reviews editor of *BBC History*, his brief biography of Mosley was published in 2004 by Haus. He is now completing a new history of the Tower of London. He lives in Sussex with his partner and three children.

Eric Midwinter is a social historian, social policy analyst and author of over fifty books on a wide range of subjects, ranging from old age and political biography to sport and comedy.

Robert Taylor is associate member of Nuffield College, Oxford and visiting fellow at Warwick University business school. He is completing a history of the Parliamentary Labour Party since 1906. He is former labour editor of *The Observer* and the *Financial Times*.

Chris Proctor has edited publications as varied as union journals and French monthlies, and his articles have (dis) graced magazines as diverse as the *Sunday Times* and *Ireland's Own*. Formerly Head of Communications at UK postal workers' and train drivers' trade unions, Chris writes a regular column for *Tribune* and features for anyone with a budget.

Paul Routledge is a columnist for the *Daily Mirror*, *Tribune* and occasionally for trade union magazines. He was political correspondent for *The Observer* and the *Independent on Sunday*, and is the author of a number of biographies including Arthur Scargill, Betty Boothroyd, John Hume, Gordon Brown, Peter Mandelson and Airey Neave. For many years he was labour editor of *The Times*, and in the 1970 general election accompanied George Brown on a barnstorming three-week tour of the country, when he came to admire and doubt Labour's 'lost leader' in about equal measure, as did many others.

Peter Cuthbertson is an account manager for a leading public affairs firm in London. Previously he worked at The Heritage Foundation, The TaxPayers' Alliance and for Conservative-Home, for which he continues to write regularly.

Anne Perkins is a writer and broadcaster. She regularly contributes editorials and comment articles to *The Guardian*, and has been a lobby correspondent for both the BBC and *Channel Four News*. She has written *Red Queen: The Authorised Biography of Barbara Castle*, *A Very British Strike*, *Baldwin* and *Little Book of Big Ideas: Politics*.

Dianne Hayter, who has a PhD in History, was the General Secretary of the Fabian Society and of the European Parliamentary Labour Party, and Chair of the Labour Party's NEC. She has published books on Labour history and helped on Denis Healey's 1981 deputy leadership campaign. She's now a member of the House of Lords.

Greg Rosen is Chair of the Labour History Group and a political columnist on *The Scotsman*. He is author of *Old Labour to New* and *Serving the People*, and was the editor of the *Dictionary of Labour Biography*.

Francis Beckett's sixteen books include biographies of four Prime Ministers – Attlee, Macmillan, Blair and Brown. His most recent book is *What Did the Baby Boomers Ever Do For Us?* in which, inter alia, he regrets that the death of John Smith paved the way for the two baby boomer Prime Ministers, Blair and Brown.

Peter Beckett has worked for leading public affairs firms in Brussels, Westminster and at County Hall in London, and for the BBC in Brussels. He is now an independent consultant on EU affairs.

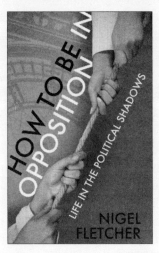